MYSTERIES LIBRARY:
DIVINATION

MYSTERIES LIBRARY:
DIVINATION

UNLOCK THE SECRETS OF ANCIENT SYMBOLS TO GAIN
FASCINATING INSIGHTS INTO YOUR LIFE AND YOUR FUTURE

WILL ADCOCK ANDY BAGGOTT STACI MENDOZA DAVID BOURNE

LORENZ BOOKS

This edition is published by Lorenz Books

Lorenz Books is an imprint of Anness Publishing Ltd
Hermes House, 88–89 Blackfriars Road, London SE1 8HA
tel. 020 7401 2077; fax 020 7633 9499
www.lorenzbooks.com; info@anness.com

© Anness Publishing Ltd 2001, 2004

UK agent: The Manning Partnership Ltd,
6 The Old Dairy, Melcombe Road, Bath BA2 3LR;
tel. 01225 478444; fax 01225 478440; sales@manning-partnership.co.uk

UK distributor: Grantham Book Services Ltd,
Isaac Newton Way, Alma Park Industrial Estate, Grantham, Lincs NG31 9SD; tel. 01476 541080; fax 01476
541061; orders@gbs.tbs-ltd.co.uk

North American agent/distributor: National Book Network,
4501 Forbes Boulevard, Suite 200, Lanham, MD 20706;
tel. 301 459 3366; fax 301 429 5746; www.nbnbooks.com

Australian agent/distributor: Pan Macmillan Australia,
Level 18, St Martins Tower, 31 Market St, Sydney, NSW 2000;
tel. 1300 135 113; fax 1300 135 103; customer.service@macmillan.com.au

New Zealand agent/distributor: David Bateman Ltd,
30 Tarndale Grove, Off Bush Road, Albany, Auckland;
tel. (09) 415 7664; fax (09) 415 8892

All rights reserved. No part of this publication may be reproduced, stored in a retrieval system, or
transmitted in any way or by any means, electronic, mechanical, photocopying, recording or otherwise,
without the prior written permission of the copyright holder.

A CIP catalogue record for this book is available from the British Library.

Publisher: Joanna Lorenz
Managing Editor: Helen Sudell
Project Editors: Emma Gray and Debra Mayhew
Designer: Axis Design
Photographers: Don Last and John Freeman
Production Controller: Claire Rae
Illustrators: Anthony Duke, Tania Monckton, Nadine Wickenden,
Sarah Young and Rebecca Yue
Editorial reader: Joy Wotton

Previously published as *Arts of Divination*

1 3 5 7 9 10 8 6 4 2

contents

introduction 6

tarot 12

i ching 38

runes 66

index 94

introduction

All writing is the embodiment of knowledge, and therefore of power for those who can interpret it. Over the centuries, the wisdom of the ancients came to be codified in complex systems of symbols. These arcane symbols of ancient shamans and mystics, whose meanings were known only to the initiated, possessed great power and became tools of psychological insight and prophecy. As the symbols were used by succeeding generations, the layers of meaning they acquired seemed to give them an intrinsic magic. By working with these symbols, it is possible to tap into ancient wisdom to gain guidance and elicit knowledge of the future.

finding your way

As you journey through life, you may sometimes find yourself in situations of confusion or doubt, prompting you to ask questions about yourself and your future. This book offers you three ways to find answers to those questions, using the Tarot, the I Ching and the runes.

All these systems of divination employ the power and magic of symbols. The images themselves can speak directly to you, whether you are looking at one of the complex illustrations of the Tarot Major Arcana or the stylized symbol of a rune. In addition, each image comes laden with the meaning that has accrued to it over centuries of use. Using the interpretations set out here, you can learn to translate these oracular pictures and symbols and see how they relate to your own life.

The origin of the Tarot is obscure. One tradition suggests that it was devised by the ancient Egyptians and written on gold leaves in a temple in Memphis. Another is that it was brought to Europe from the Middle East by returning Crusaders in the 14th century. Sometimes referred to as "The Devil's Book", the Tarot was banned at various periods in France, Germany and other countries.

The 22 cards of the Major Arcana, or "greater secrets", relate to the most important issues in your life and take precedence in a reading. They fall into three groups, representing the concerns of the material world, the intuitive mind and the realm

of change. The cards of the Minor Arcana, or "lesser secrets", refer to more everyday situations, while the four court cards in each suit – the page, knight, queen and king – represent people who have some influence over your life. While divination is possible using only the cards of the Major Arcana, the inclusion of the Minor Arcana will refine the reading and result in a more comprehensive interpretation.

intuition ancient wisdom

Some Tarot readers attach different interpretations to the cards if they appear upside down in a spread: for this reason it is important to make sure that all the cards in the pack are upright before a reading begins, so that any reversals occur only as a result of the querent handling the cards. Both "upright" and "reversed" meanings are given for each card. However, you should not feel that you must slavishly follow any of the interpretations given here once your intuition starts to lead you in a particular direction: it is important to allow the images to speak directly to you on an intuitive level if you are to gain a true insight into your inner self, or into that of someone else for whom you are giving a reading. With experience, each reader will develop his or her own unique approach to the Tarot.

The I Ching, or "Book of Changes" originated in China over 4,000 years ago. It is based on 64 systematic symbols known as hexagrams, which are six-lined figures made up of the symbols for yin (a broken line) and yang (a continuous line) in all their possible combinations. Each line of the hexagram is determined by the casting of lots, usually in the form of coins, to produce a series of even (yin) or odd (yang) numbers.

The purpose of casting the coins is to divine the rising and falling of positive or negative influences – the yin and yang (or two sides) of the universe. In Chinese philosophy, these two opposing principles are the basis of the whole of creation. The ancient seers observed the natural rhythms and cycles of the world, watching the ebb and flow of the tides, the changing of the seasons and the transition from day into night. They concluded that everything was in a constant state of flux produced by two opposing and absolute forces.

The ancient meaning of yin was the cool, shady, north side of a hill, while yang was the hot, sunny, south side. The first six months of the year are traditionally seen as yang, a time of masculine activity such as hunting, building and farming. The later part of the

year is more yin, a time of weaving, childbirth and planning for the year ahead. Yin is perceived as a female quality, soft and still, identified with the mystery of the night, the earth and the moon. Yang is male, active and hard and controls the heavens and the sun. Everything, including humanity itself, is subject to these two polarities, and harmony in life is achieved by balancing one against the other.

Yin and yang are definite opposites, but the evolution of the six-lined symbols allowed subtle gradations between the two to be represented. Further layers of meaning were introduced into the I Ching by adding interpretations to each individual "changing" line. These are lines which, when cast, represent extreme yin or yang and are therefore transformed into their opposite, since each polarity contains the germ of the other.

By asking a question of the I Ching, you can build an understanding of those things that are good for your personal growth as well as those things that are limiting your progress. A consultation should be accompanied by ritual and meditation to quieten your thoughts and open your mind to the counsel given by the oracle.

The runes are an ancient magical tool of northern Europe. Their name means both "secret" and "whisper", and each one carries a message which can be used in meditation, for guidance or for personal protection.

The lore of the runes is linked with Norse mythology, and the runes themselves were said to have been brought to earth by Odin, the father of the gods. His wisdom and his ability to foretell the ultimate doom of the gods were the result of his shamanic initiation, which took the form of self-sacrifice. Odin hanged himself upside-down on the branches of the tree of knowledge, Yggdrasil, for nine days and nights – an event which is echoed in the image of the Hanged Man in the Tarot pack. Through his suffering and death Odin was endowed with the wisdom embodied in the runes, and the indomitable will he showed in his pursuit of knowledge led to his rebirth. The runes were his gift to humanity.

consultation

The interpretation of the runes was the prerogative of the runemasters, shamans who, like Odin, had passed through rites of initiation to gain wisdom. They used the runes for divination, healing and magic. The runic alphabet was also used in inscriptions until the 19th century, and some elements were assimilated into Scandinavian languages, but the runes are now used exclusively as aids to divination.

To get to know the runes intimately, and to benefit from working with them, it is important that your set should be truly personal to you, and the best way to achieve this is to make them yourself. Runes are usually made from either stone or wood, and in either case the collection of the materials should be approached with reverence and ritual to preserve their natural vibrations. The work and care involved in the act of carving or painting the symbols will help you set up a close relationship with them, which will develop as you consult and care for your runes.

It is necessary to approach a consultation of the runes with your mind open and calm, so that you can access your intuitive response to their message. This book includes guidance on using meditation as a way to quieten your thoughts and, while holding a single rune, to tune in to its vibration. A number of runes can be used in a variety of different spreads, each of which will help in its own way to give you an insight into your situation and direct you on your spiritual path. Sample readings are provided for each of these. As you develop your relationship with a particular rune – your personal rune – you may find it helpful to research the tree, colour, herb and crystal which corresponds with it, each of which has healing properties that can be of special benefit to you.

Like the Tarot and the I Ching, using the runes as tools of divination will not provide simple answers to all your problems, but a consultation can help you to find your personal gifts and powers, and can also help you strengthen your resolve as you travel your spiritual path.

tarot

For hundreds of years, the Tarot has been a source of mystery and fascination, intriguing us with its compelling and enigmatic pictures and symbols. No one really knows where the Tarot originated, or how or why it works, but if we can "tune in" to the images we can gain access to a deeper understanding of ourselves and the people and events involved in our lives.

The Tarot deck is composed of 78 cards, which divide into two parts: the 22 cards of the Major Arcana and the 56 cards, in four suits, of the Minor Arcana, which closely parallels a normal pack of playing cards. The Major Arcana reflects the major turning points in our lives: our commitments, triumphs and tragedies, while the cards of the Minor Arcana deal with the more day-to-day aspects of life. Together, they constitute a guide to the incidents and issues that we have to handle.

This section provides a concise guide to the Tarot, with a general definition of each card. It also suggests different tarot spreads and ways in which you can use this ancient system of divination to give readings for yourself and others. Although there are general guidelines to the meaning of the cards, the ultimate aim is for you to develop your intuitive skills using the Tarot and to arrive at your own conclusions. In the end, each reader and their interpretation is as unique as a set of finger-prints. The Tarot still has the potential to be original and fresh and perhaps this is why it is as popular today as it was centuries ago.

aspects of the tarot

The Tarot is designed to relate, pictorially, what you are feeling inside. It reflects your psychological and emotional state as well as showing you the people and events involved in your life. You should use the images on the cards as a springboard, allowing their intuitive meaning to come through. However, while you are new to the Tarot, the following general guidelines can be applied to your reading of the cards.

Major Arcana

There are 21 numbered cards in the Major Arcana, plus the unnumbered Fool. The 21 cards represent states which affect everyone at some time. As the Major Arcana cards are so significant, they will always take special precedence in a Tarot spread.

The cards of the Major Arcana can be broken down into three groups, each consisting of seven cards. The first deals with the realm of the material world: material comforts, the choices that reflect and influence physical life, and higher education.

The second group deals with the realm of the intuitive mind. This covers aspects such as faith, free will, love and its transforming effect, and psychic understanding.

The third group is concerned with the combination of the first two and forms the realm of changing issues. It contains the most significant and powerful cards in the entire deck as they have the added bonus of challenging or altering the path of life you are actually on.

Astrology also plays a part in the composition of the Tarot deck. The sun, the moon, the twelve signs of the zodiac and the planets of the solar system are all reflected within the cards of the Major Arcana. The four suits of the Minor Arcana have astrological associations with the four classical elements of astrology: earth, air, fire and water.

Minor Arcana

Although it is possible to do Tarot readings using only the Major Arcana cards, the story would not really be complete without the 56 cards of the Minor Arcana. This group of cards completes the balance by showing the finer and more ordinary details of our lives, such as the people you know, places you frequent, particular events and day-to-day circumstances.

The Minor Arcana is broken down into four separate suits of 14 cards each. These are Cups, Wands, Pentacles and Swords, which correspond to Hearts, Clubs, Diamonds and Spades in an ordinary deck of playing cards. Their numerical order runs from ace to ten (pip cards), with four court cards – Page, Knight, Queen and King – to complete the sequence. Some modern tarot decks use cards called the Prince and Princess instead of the Page and Knight.

Each of the four suits deals with a different, yet equally significant, area or aspect of life. The suit of Cups deals with emotions and issues that are concerned with love and relationships. The suit of Wands deals with physical actions and activities and ambitions. The suit of Pentacles deals with all aspects of security, such as finance, your career, home and family. Finally, the suit of Swords deals with moral issues and the conflicts that can arise as a result.

While the cards of the Major Arcana reflect issues that have a dramatic impact, daily life is more likely to be made up of lots of little areas and incidents, some of which can seem quite boring or insignificant. These are shown by the Minor Arcana. It is by combining the two distinct parts of the Tarot deck that you can arrive at a more in-depth and realistic interpretation of your life and its circumstances.

Reading the Cards

The symbolism and meanings given here reflect a popular and traditional point of view. They represent an overview of the basic imagery that has been present in many forms in the cards during their history. Today there are hundreds of Tarot decks, each with their own vision and ideas about the Tarot. However, although a lot of decks will look very different to those shown here, in most cases these general descriptions will remain valid.

When you buy a new Tarot pack, all the cards will come in numerical and sequential order. For the purpose of learning each card's definition, it is probably useful to follow this order. Once the definitions have been mastered, however, there is no need to keep the cards in any particular order.

Some people like to distinguish between upright and reversed directions when the cards are laid out in a spread. The reversed direction can significantly alter the meaning of the card.

Aces

The Ace is the crowning card in any deck. Mathematically valued as either one or 11, it can be used to win card games because of its mathematical duality. This theme of winning or victory is also present in the Tarot, and Aces are usually seen as extremely positive cards and as the keystones of the Minor Arcana.

The Aces contain the powerful energy of the entire suit that they represent, the absolute truth of that particular element, whether it is earth, air fire or water. They are of great help when approaching any new or difficult situation. The Ace cards are from the suits of Wands, Pentacles, Cups and Swords. The Major Arcana has no Ace card but the unnumbered Fool takes up its place in this grouping.

Eights

The Eights have a special role and are particularly important in a reading. This is because the figure 8 relates to the symbol of infinity, the never-ending cycle in which all lives spiral, always constant yet always changing. Any of the Eights will therefore highlight changes in your life, or the sense of moving forward. These cards are the eighth Major Arcana card, which will be called Strength or Justice depending on the pack, and the Eights in the suits of Wands, Pentacles, Cups and Swords in the Minor Arcana.

Fool

The only oddity of the Major Arcana is the Fool, whose number is zero. In medieval times, the Fool held a special place in society. For many people, he was an innocent in contact with the gods and was able to say and do more or less anything he liked. It is this idea that held sway and influenced the card imagery of the Fool when the Tarot was developed, and thus the Fool jumped into the Major Arcana in its own unique and individual way.

The Fool does not fit into any of the three sections of seven in the Major Arcana, so it can be placed either at the beginning or at the end of the Major group, in a similar way to the Aces of the Minor Suits. This decision is traditionally left to the individual, but for the purposes of this book and for learning the Major Arcana definitions, the Fool has been placed at the beginning.

Traditionally, the Fool is represented as a young, androgynous figure with a look of wonder in his eyes. In some decks he is sniffing a beautiful rose so intently that he does not notice he is just about to step over a dangerous cliff. The figure carries a staff with a bag attached to it, while at his heels a white animal snaps, almost as if it is trying to force the character over the edge of the precipice. The Fool is seen as an adventurous card and the feeling of change is often associated with it.

Pages

In former times, pages were young men and boys who worked in the royal courts, bringing messages, notices and letters and running errands. They served at table, helped the lords and ladies of the court to dress and did a multitude of other things. Being a page was the young person's education for a good position in life, and might eventually lead to a knighthood if they served well. In the Tarot deck, the Pages are not specifically male or female. They can represent some or all of the following elements: children, messages, communication (which may now include telephone calls, letters, e-mails or any other medium), information being given and passed on, studying or apprenticeship.

Knights

In the days of chivalry, knights were men who served the king and his court. They were sent out on errands, to find new lands, make new discoveries, forge new ties and test their skills. In the Tarot, the Knights are figures of action; they take up quests – whether the goal is self-discovery and finding your purpose in life, or challenging misfortune and injustice on behalf of others. In today's society, where both men and women share the workplace and life's responsibilities, it is important to remember that Knights can be male or female.

Queen

The queen was considered to fulfill a role as the mature partner of the king, rather than as a ruler on her own account. In the Tarot deck, the Queen is a symbol of feminine power rather than imperious royalty. She can be both bride and mother. The Queen primarily represents women, and spheres of interest that have traditionally been associated with women: the home, relationships and emotional nurturing. A Queen can also represent a man who exhibits qualities or concerns in these areas.

King

The king was the ruler of the land, and his duty was to maintain law and order and preserve the safety of his kingdom. In the Tarot, the King is the symbol of masculine power, self-assertion and creative energy. Kings will primarily represent men and those spheres of interest that have traditionally been associated with men in a position of power and authority: ruling, responsibility and decision-making. A King can also represent a woman who exhibits qualities or concerns in these areas.

major arcana: the material world

The seven cards in the first group of the Major Arcana deal with situations that are connected to commitment through society's laws, such as marriage, success, higher education and the family. The Fool, numbered zero, begins this sequence, although he is sometimes placed last in the sequence of the Major Arcana, before or after the World.

0 the fool

planet Uranus

The fool is portrayed as a youthful figure dressed in particoloured clothes, sometimes with the cap and bells of the court jester. He carries a staff, representing his willpower, from which hangs a bag containing his worldly goods. A small animal, usually a dog, is often shown snapping aggressively at his heels. The animal is said to stand for the world of instinct. The fool is the agent of luck, always ready to change, and this is an adventurous card.

Upright
Spontaneity and a new beginning. New experiences will bring excitement, so accept the process of change. You will be taking a risk or an unknown step forwards.

Reversed
Venturing out without thinking results in frequent mistakes, so evaluate matters before going ahead. This could indicate a reluctance to accept responsibility.

1 the magician

planet Mercury

A man stands before a table as if he is about to perform a demonstration. His left hand is raised, pointing upwards towards the sky. In it he holds a wand. His right hand is holding a coin, but lowered, pointing towards the ground. Before him on the table lies a sword, a cup, a wand and a pentacle (or coin). Above his head there is an infinity symbol and surrounding him are flowers and other greenery.

Upright
This card warns you to bring all aspects of your life together: love, emotions, finances and morality. This is to prepare for changes and handle them well.

Reversed
An individual who conducts her/himself with great presence and perfectionism and who appears always to handle chaotic situations with ease.

II the high priestess

the Moon

A woman in long, richly coloured, draped robes sits on a throne. Above her hangs a veil which sometimes has a flowing stream running behind it. The woman holds a book and often wears the symbol of the crescent moon, identifying her with the Egyptian goddess Isis. The High Priestess is also sometimes known as the Female Pope and symbolizes virginity.

Upright
Trust your intuition. Don't take things at face value. Look for answers to your questions within your heart. Use logic less to come to the right answer.

Reversed
Everything is out in the open, nothing is hidden and all the facts are obvious. You will now be able to make your decision, using both intuition and logic.

III the empress

The Empress is represented by a voluptuous woman clothed in a long flowing dress and smiling serenely. She wears a crown and holds a sceptre and a protective shield with the symbol of an eagle. She is normally depicted in natural surroundings, with a stream flowing behind her. She represents security and motherhood.

planet Venus

Upright
The card to indicate fertility or pregnancy. For those beyond child-bearing years, it means domestic bliss.

Reversed
A woman who loves to care for others, though it can mean domestic disharmony.

IV the emperor

The Emperor is an older man sitting on an unseen throne. In his left hand he holds a sceptre and in his right he holds an imperial orb with a cross on it, which is a sign of authority. Sometimes he has a large eagle on his hat. He signifies a male influence, with confidence and worldly power, and a person well capable of using authority.

sign of Aries

Upright
Any established organization (bank, school, government office). It may mean you are trying to establish a company.

Reversed
Disarray or conflict with organizations. Take action and point out problems.

V the hierophant

Also known as the "High Priest", this figure is the male counterpart of the High Priestess. He also sits between two pillars, dressed like a churchman with a triple papal crown. He offers a benediction with his right hand and holds a sceptre with a cross on the top. Before him kneel two pleading supplicants.

sign of Taurus

Upright
The need for professional advice, or ritual, such as marriage, christening, or divorce.

Reversed
Someone who follows rules, perhaps an accountant or doctor. It also represents a stable and successful individual.

VI the lovers

A young man stands at a crossroads, and on each path a woman waits. The fair-haired woman stands on the right and the dark-haired on the left. Above the man flies Cupid or an angel, offering him the choice of either of these two paths. This card usually indicates love or possibly the beginning of a romance.

sign of Gemini

Upright
Instant chemistry in an intimate relationship formed by a chance meeting.

Reversed
Someone who challenges society's rules regarding gender roles, and will not fit a stereotype.

VII the chariot

A strong-looking male figure rides in a chariot pulled by two sphinxes or sometimes two horses. In many decks the sphinx, or horse, on the right-hand side is light in colour and the one on the left is dark, representing good and evil. In the man's right hand there is a wand or sceptre. The canopy of the chariot is covered in stars.

sign of Cancer

Upright
A victory against the odds. There are many obstacles, but you feel that you are right.

Reversed
At this time, it would be unwise to apply any more pressure to the situation concerned. If you do, you risk pushing people or circumstances over the limit.

major arcana: the intuitive mind

The second group of seven Major Arcana cards focuses more on the individual than on society and worldly concerns. Decisions about the issues with which these cards are concerned are based more on how you feel than on what you think. This section deals with circumstances that really touch your heart, such as the search for personal faith, love and justice.

VIII justice

sign of Libra

A woman, who is identified with the Greek goddess of justice, sits on a throne. In her right hand she holds a set of scales and in her left a great double-edged sword. She is often blindfolded. This card indicates fairness and balance, the need to be logical and diplomatic and to argue in a balanced way. It can also refer to sustaining the balance of nature. In some decks, this card may appear as number 11, with Strength as number 8.

Upright
Justice will be served in the settling of an issue. A very favourable card in a karmic sense. Whatever the outcome of a particular situation, it will be a fair one.

Reversed
An injustice will take place. The outcome of a particular circumstance will be unfair. This reversed card can also indicate bias and a lack of balance in a situation.

IX the hermit

planet Jupiter

An old man with a dowager's hump who wears the dark robes of a monk. In one hand he holds a staff to support himself and in his other hand he holds a lighted lantern which he shines on the path before him. In some decks, the light from the lantern emits rays of light that resemble the beams of a star. The Hermit represents the wisdom of age, using his lantern to light the path towards self-enlightenment.

Upright
This is a preparation card, warning you to bring all the elements of your life together – emotions, action, finances and morality – to enable you to handle the changes ahead correctly.

Reversed
An individual who always appears to be "together". A person who handles difficult circumstances with ease.

X the wheel of fortune

sign of Virgo

There is a wheel in the centre of the card with Fortune in the middle. In some decks the letters TARO are written upon the wheel in the position of the four cardinal points – north, south, east and west – as if the wheel were a compass. Sometimes figures or animals climb up the outside of the wheel. In this deck at the top of the wheel on a platform is a sphinx; in other decks it is often a man with ass's ears. The card indicates destiny and fate.

Upright
Fate will take a strong hand and redirect your path. The change may be good or bad. What you do after this redirection is in your own hands.

Reversed
Although you may have experienced a run of bad luck, this card indicates that things are changing and your life will be soon taking a turn for the better.

XI strength

In most decks, the strength or fortitude card is illustrated by a young man or woman controlling a lion in some manner. Some cards show Hercules killing the Nemean lion, whose skin he will wear to make himself invincible. The card indicates not only physical strength but also moral fortitude, self-discipline and courage. In some decks Strength appears as number 8 and Justice appears as number 11.

sign of Leo

Upright

There is no need to worry, or lose sight of your goals. Even if the road you are on is difficult, you will get there in the end. Be patient and persevere. Have confidence.

Reversed

You feel a need to seek reassurance from a trusted source to help you get back on the right track. Re-evaluate your position and consider where you are going.

XII the hanged man

A young man hangs from a tree by his left leg. His right leg is folded behind the left, making a shape like the number four. His arms are folded behind his back. The man's face does not look tortured but quite serene. The image represents a sacrifice of some kind which results in a transformation. It is identified with the Norse god Odin, who hanged himself from the World Tree in order to gain wisdom, and was reborn.

planet Neptune

Upright

Life is at a standstill. Although things may not be to your liking, it is not as bad as you think. Take life patiently until you see that the time is right to make the necessary improvements to your situation.

Reversed

A great contentment in life. You are feeling so happy with your present situation that you almost feel blissful.

XIII death

A skeletal figure wields either a bow or a large scythe. The ground he walks across is cracked, and in some decks he is walking through a field of bones and cutting off the heads of figures that have been buried up to their necks in the earth. Generally this card's meaning is not a negative one: it indicates getting rid of the old to make way for the new, or a time of change and renewal after a loss or an ordeal.

sign of Scorpio

Upright

Regeneration and rebirth, a new outlook on life. Sometimes this occurs after an unparalleled event has taken place, such as a near-death experience.

Reversed

A refusal to let change happen, or a situation end. This can lead to a deep depression which may create the need to seek advice from a doctor or counsellor.

XIV temperance

An angel-like figure holds a cup in each hand, from which she pours liquid, one into the other. Sometimes a pool of water is shown in which the angel has one foot placed in the pool and one foot placed on land. The card indicates moderation and the blending of opposites. The image of Temperance symbolizes balance, harmony and moderation, and another aspect of its meaning concerns the healing effects of time.

sign of Sagittarius

Upright

You need to test the waters first, not dive into the middle of a situation without thinking. Be patient and take things nice and slowly. Go carefully "where angels fear to tread". Exert some self-control.

Reversed

This indicates that it is time to re-evaluate the situation before you proceed so you do not make the same mistakes again.

major arcana: the realm of change

The seven cards of the final group of the Major Arcana are the most revered of all the Major cards because they go beyond the realm of society and the concern of the individual. They represent those universal laws and issues that have the power to bring about the kind of circumstances and events that can alter the course and path of all our lives.

XV the devil

sign of Capricorn

A large figure, half-human and half-beast in appearance, stands on a pedestal. He has a female torso and the legs of a goat, though they may be covered in scales. He also has horns and the wings of a bat or bird. Two other figures with horns, who may be a man and a woman or are sometimes lesser devils, are bound to the pedestal on which the devil is standing by heavy ropes around their necks, and stand on either side of him.

Upright
This challenging card indicates new-found passions, together with energy and enthusiasm. Rediscovering your innermost self and having the impetus to act on them.

Reversed
Obsessions, addictions, and compulsive behaviour. When passion is directed in a negative manner, seeing a given situation with clarity is almost impossible.

XVI the tower

planet Mars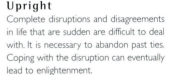

An apparently strongly built, impregnable high tower is being struck by a lightning bolt. This may be a dramatic and unforeseeable natural disaster, or the lightning may have been sent by an angry god as a punishment for the presumption of the tower's builders. As a result of the explosion, fire leaps from the tower and the top begins to crumble. One or more figures are falling to their doom at the base of the building.

Upright
Complete disruptions and disagreements in life that are sudden are difficult to deal with. It is necessary to abandon past ties. Coping with the disruption can eventually lead to enlightenment.

Reversed
The worst disruptions are over and it is time to put your life back together in a way that is more suitable and positive.

XVII the star

sign of Aquarius

A multitude of stars are shining in the night sky above a woman. This card shows a naked woman kneeling beside a pool or stream. She holds two cups in her hands. From one cup she pours water on to the land and from the other she pours it back into the pool. Resembling Venus, the goddess of beauty, she revives the land with the water from the pool, while the morning star heralds the beginning of a new dawn.

Upright
A wish come true, usually something you have hoped for since you were a child, such as meeting the perfect partner or the ideal career opportunity.

Reversed
What once seemed like a dream come true is no longer appealing. Now that you have your desire, you become filled with self-doubt and wonder if it was worth it.

XVIII the moon

sign of Pisces

Two dogs, one dark and one light in colour, bay up at a large shining moon. In other decks a woman holds a crescent moon. There may be a pool of water in the foreground, in which swims a crab. This is the emblem of Cancer, the astrological sign associated with the moon. The dogs suggest a connection with Anubis, the jackal-headed Egyptian god who presided over the dead and conducted souls into the afterlife.

Upright
Someone or something is not what it seems. There is a risk here that you are being lied to. Take another look at the situation and ask more questions.

Reversed
Lies or deceptions are being practised. It would be best to become detached from a particular person or situation at this time because neither is likely to change.

XIX the sun

the Sun

In this very positive image, a large yellow sun shines down on a verdant garden of flowers in which two children or young people are playing or sitting talking together. The sun is a positive force of illumination, presaging good fortune, health, happiness and worldly success. It promotes growth and inspires vitality and confidence. However, if it is too bright it can also dazzle and blind you to the truth of a situation.

Upright
A very positive card indicating growth and increased potential, such as progression in relationships, financial expansion, and physical growth (as in pregnancy).

Reversed
See your life for what it is and not what you think it is. Re-evaluate your situation to make better progress and have a clearer sense of purpose and direction.

XX judgement

planet Pluto

An angel flies above the earth blowing a trumpet. On the earth below, people rise from a tomb with their arms and hands held open towards the sky. In some decks, a godly figure appears at the top of the picture. This card, portraying a vision of the Day of Judgement, symbolizes an end of a situation and then rejuvenation and regeneration. It may indicate that this is a good time to make a profound change in your life to free yourself from restrictions.

Upright
An indication that what has been holding you up is ending. You are free to move forwards with a more positive attitude. The lifting of karmic restrictions.

Reversed
Poor judgement. This could keep you at a standstill or in a rut if you are not careful about the choices you make at this point. Take time to evaluate your direction.

XXI the world

planet Saturn

A hermaphroditic figure dances lightly as if on air. In both hands she holds white wands, while around her there is a wreath or halo without a join. From all four corners of the card the same beasts that are present on the Wheel of Fortune card look inwards towards the dancing figure. They are the creatures associated with the four fixed signs of the zodiac. In some decks, this card shows two children supporting a globe-like object.

Upright
This is by far the most auspicious card in the deck. It indicates great success for the individual in all areas of life.

Reversed
A fear of your own success in life. It is as though the goal is within reach, but you hesitate to take it – perhaps through fear of it not being quite deserved or fear of being disappointed.

minor arcana: swords

When the Swords are present in a reading, the issues that are indicated by this suit concern any situations or actions to do with morality, moral conflict and conflicts in general. Think of an actual sword. It is sharply pointed, double-edged and made of strong metal, such as steel. The suit of Swords is related to the element of air. It equates to the suit of Spades in a pack of playing cards.

ace of swords

Upright
Victory and triumph after some difficulties and hard work. This time you have really achieved and it's been you alone who has done all the work. When the victory comes, it cannot be taken away. Well-deserved success.

Reversed
You must not put any more pressure on to a person or situation as you are in danger of pushing things over the edge. It would be best to sit back and allow the person or situation to calm down for a while, even though such a delay may be frustrating for you.

four of swords

Upright
This card indicates that you need to take some time out to rest, recover and recuperate. This is in order to gather your energies for a difficult situation that has just arisen or lies ahead. You need to concentrate on pacing yourself.

Reversed
You may have been suffering from an illness or fatigue brought on by a difficult situation, but now you have rested you are ready to take on life and its challenges again. You are able to enter the rat-race once more.

two of swords

Upright
Imposed self-protection, a wall is being put up between you and the outside world. This is usually due to your experience of upsetting situations which have caused you to build up your defences to guard against the pain.

Reversed
You are too overprotective and not allowing anyone to get close. Be more open-minded.

five of swords

Upright
A rift or argument has happened and you must deal with this before your relationship can move forward. You have succeeded in proving an important point and your opinion has been noted.

Reversed
Now you have made your point successfully, there is no need to be petulant about the issue and rub salt into the wounds or you could be accused of being ruthless.

three of swords

Upright
You may experience heartache through a love triangle: for example you, your husband and your lover or you, your mother and your sister. Someone, if not all three people, will get hurt through choices that need to be made.

Reversed
Heartache through a love triangle as for the upright position, but on a less serious scale, such as disagreements, slight jealousies and insecurities, that can more easily be resolved.

six of swords

Upright
You are moving out of rough times in your life. Your situation or emotions will change. Life is on the up and you will be able to deal with problems more easily. Perseverance will still be needed, however, if you are to gain your objectives.

Reversed
When it is reversed, this card could indicate a delay in your change of fortune, or that your situation is improving, but not quite so smoothly or as quickly as you would like it to.

seven of swords

Upright
Through your pride in your capabilities, or because you do not know how to say "no", you are taking on more than you can handle. Be vigilant and avoid becoming over-stressed.

Reversed
Certain pressures or problems that you have been experiencing in your life up to this point are beginning to ease up.

eight of swords

Upright
There are restrictions on your ability to get on with your life freely, such as living with a possessive partner, strict parents or being restricted through disability, pregnancy, culture or faith.

Reversed
The feelings of frustration or the restrictions that have been imposed on you are being lifted, enabling you to move on.

nine of swords

Upright
You are suffering from intense worries or stresses. You feel overwhelmed by these anxieties which you have been carrying alone. You need to explain your troubles to another person to make them more bearable.

Reversed
The stresses or worries have intensified, leading to anxiety and fear. This is quite a serious problem and you have reached a stage where it would be best to seek professional guidance.

ten of swords

Upright
Your feelings have already been deeply hurt as a result of a situation or person. This will have been a painful experience for you but you will bear it in the knowledge that it will come to an end and you will get it out of your system.

Reversed
This card has a very negative meaning when it is reversed, indicating a period of grief for you. Great pain or heartache will be inflicted on you intentionally by a person or situation.

page of swords

Upright
A wonderful feeling of enthusiasm, excitement and a desire to make a fresh start and take life head-on will come over you and make you feel as though it is New Year's Day again.

Reversed
A person you know is behaving frantically and impulsively, usually as a result of great excitement.

knight of swords

Upright
An individual with great determination, but also of great loyalty, conviction and strength of character. They will diligently pursue their aims while respecting and caring for others.

Reversed
A person whose zeal has led him or her to behave brashly, at times stepping on other people's feelings.

queen of swords

Upright
This woman is often a leader in her family or social group carrying the moral load. She can be stubborn but is deeply loyal to her loved ones. Her general demeanour is of someone strong and reliable, yet possibly a little aloof or distant.

Reversed
In outward appearance she is very similar to the upright Queen, but when reversed she can become extreme, judgemental and stubborn. She can come across as being cold and aloof.

king of swords

Upright
A man who will often have a fixed routine. He has a strong sense of responsibility and strong loyalties: he would rather suffer than let other people down. He is sensible, yet also emotional.

Reversed
A man who can be overly regimented and military in his routines. He is also rather harsh and cruel in his judgements, with a narrow outlook on life. Intolerance and narrow-mindedness are the key factors of this card.

minor arcana: wands

The issues that happen under this suit are connected with physical activity and action. Wands are concerned with the "here and now" and there is usually a lot of hubbub and activity surrounding them. Wands indicate a creative energy and an extrovert quality. They are also associated with intuition. The suit of Wands is related to the element of fire. It equates to the suit of Clubs in a pack of playing cards.

ace of wands

Upright
Put quite simply, the time to act on an idea is now! If you are planning any ventures or special tasks, now is the right time to get things moving. Karmically speaking, this time is most auspicious for the future of any given project or issue.

Reversed
Plans are currently put on hold or there is a lack of interest. Although it may be frustrating to wait, it is not the right time to proceed. It is better to wait until the timing feels right.

two of wands

Upright
Now is a good time to bring new people into your life and to share what you have to offer through friendship and lifestyle. This can increase your happiness and give meaning to your life.

Reversed
Someone who is living the life of a hermit and not finding happiness in that lifestyle. Now is the time to take drastic measures to become socially involved by taking up activities that have a varied group of people. The alternative is to face living life alone.

three of wands

Upright
It is time to pursue new directions in life. A new path is opening up and if you go down it, it will bring positive things into your life. This could indicate, for example, taking up higher learning or beginning to research a subject that interests you.

Reversed
You are being too passive, waiting for life to happen to you. It is time to formulate new ideas about the path that you can follow. Decide what it is you are interested in and take action.

four of wands

Upright
There is a warm and festive feeling in your life. Now is a good time to emphasize your feeling of goodwill by getting friends and family together to share in these positive vibrations. This could be through an informal get-together, such as a weekend away, a barbecue, a picnic, or a party.

Reversed
You feel fed up. You need to take physical action, such as changing your scenery by taking a holiday or redecorating your home.

five of wands

Upright
Discussions are taking place at the moment to clear the air on certain subjects. Usually these debates are beneficial and can lead to greater harmony between the parties involved.

Reversed
This card indicates that there is a degree of discord in current discussions or negotiations, which is causing all suggestions to hit a blank wall. Consequently, the matter that is under discussion will require time and patience before it is resolved.

six of wands

Upright
You will receive public recognition as a result of a job that is well done. Your peer group and those closest to you give you support for your actions. You feel satisfied with your efforts.

Reversed
This indicates that you will receive the recognition that has long been due to you for a good deed or achievement. Now you will be given adequate thanks for your efforts and will be able to look back on it with satisfaction.

seven of wands

Upright
You will need to protect and defend your current position. It is time to watch out for the competition in a personal or professional capacity, but you should have no problems.

Reversed
This card shows that you doubt yourself. You are in danger of being caught off-guard in a personal or professional capacity.

eight of wands

Upright
Life is moving in the fast lane. See which cards fall next to this card, as their course of action will be speeded up. For example, the World next to the Eight would mean that success is imminent.

Reversed
Things are grinding to a halt, or you feel misdirected. Re-evaluate your current position before pushing ahead with new ideas.

nine of wands

Upright
There is a chance that you are being overly defensive or suspicious, even paranoid about a person, event or situation that is currently important to you. It is best to examine your feelings carefully before you react.

Reversed
Your suspicions have been verified and it is time to move on in your life. The best advice is to look to the future and not to get too engrossed or involved in the problems of the past.

ten of wands

Upright
You are currently going through a lot of stresses and strains. You have many responsibilities at the moment, but you are quite capable of handling them, so don't worry too much about coming through this period successfully.

Reversed
The intense strains of recent times have started to subside and you are beginning to feel more relaxed and contented. This card reversed may also indicate the loss of someone close to you.

page of wands

Upright
The Page indicates news coming to you, for example, by post, telephone, or e-mail. It is information that will be of special interest and significance.

Reversed
Precisely the same as the definition for an upright position, except that the news or information you receive will be coming from someone who is younger than yourself.

knight of wands

Upright
A person who is soul-searching. Until they find the answers, do not try to pin them down. Wait and you will be rewarded with a life-long friend.

Reversed
A person chaotically looking for answers. Such chaos can lead to outbursts of temper from someone who is too extreme in their passions.

queen of wands

Upright
A woman who has a deep desire to be the centre of attention. She is charismatic and knows how to use her charms in order to better herself. She is often exotic in appearance and good with her hands as well as her mind.

Reversed
When reversed, the Queen becomes competitive and manipulative in order to be the centre of attention. She puts more value on what she can win for herself than on people.

king of wands

Upright
A man who is non-judgemental, with a welcoming and giving nature devoid of any competitive streak. He prefers to be close to nature in order to feel grounded in life. In appearance, he is as relaxed as his personality.

Reversed
When reversed, the king is rather eccentric. He does not have good "people skills" and he does not understand humanity and its blatant vulgarity. He can appear intolerant or narrow-minded.

minor arcana: pentacles

The pentacle is a gold disc that symbolizes money, and the issues that fall under this suit are to do with security and the material elements of life, such as career, investments, family, marriage, children, home, and any of those things that give us security or a sense of belonging. The suit of Pentacles is related to the element of earth. It equates to the suit of Diamonds in a pack of playing cards.

ace of pentacles

Upright
Great rewards or success concerning a security issue. This could be a sudden windfall or the feeling of finally achieving success in your career. This is also the card to indicate total success in a relationship, suggesting security and contentment.

Reversed
This card indicates a reversal of fortune that involves your financial situation or a relationship. This is a time of feeling "at your lowest point" and of experiencing the inner emptiness.

two of pentacles

Upright
You need to keep up your balancing act for a little while longer. Don't make any decision to drop any one aspect of your life just yet: you will need to wait for some more information before making that choice.

Reversed
You are in a situation that is difficult to control. A greater degree of flexibility may help. Assessing, then organizing your priorities would give you a considerable advantage at a time like this.

three of pentacles

Upright
The three of Pentacles represents a signature on contracts or some other important paperwork. This could mean that you will be signing a document such as a marriage certificate, an employment contract, mortgage or divorce papers.

Reversed
There will be a delay in signing contracts or official documents at this time, and this could lead you to feel very frustrated. When this card is reversed, it can also be a sign of impending quarrels.

four of pentacles

Upright
You have some real fears about finances and feel the need to hold on to your money. Perhaps you have experienced financial stresses that have left you feeling insecure.

Reversed
You may feel deeply insecure in financial matters from a real cause in the past. It has left you fearful of spending money even when you are financially secure. Pay attention to emotional matters and do not lose sight of what is truly important.

five of pentacles

Upright
This card warns of a financial disaster or serious loss of security of some kind that has occurred recently or else is on the way. This insecurity may be as a result of losing your job, bankruptcy or general money losses of some kind.

Reversed
The financial or security loss has already taken place and you may feel a sense of helplessness. The task of putting things back together should not be put off any longer.

six of pentacles

Upright
You will be looked after or treated fairly regarding a security issue. An indication of generosity in a financial way, such things as a pay rise, a profitable house sale, a generous divorce or court settlement, for example.

Reversed
You may receive unfair treatment around a security issue – such as a well-deserved pay rise, divorce, house sale or a legal settlement. You are not happy about the outcome.

seven of pentacles

Upright
Now is a good time to spoil yourself or make an investment and get the benefits of your hard work. This would not have any adverse effect on your finances at this time.

Reversed
It is time to stop "saving up for a rainy day". This attitude towards your finances is no longer appropriate: treat yourself.

eight of pentacles

Upright
You have a talent with your hands that could earn you financial rewards and could become a career. This card refers to any person who works with their hands.

Reversed
You have talent, but it needs fine tuning. Practise your skill, so that you become able enough to proceed with a proper career.

nine of pentacles

Upright
This card represents a woman whose natural demeanour attracts a good lifestyle. She looks competent and well groomed. If she has a partner, he is most likely to be successful.

Reversed
When the card is reversed, it indicates a woman who can employ ruthless methods in obtaining a satisfactory lifestyle for herself. She may marry a man for his money, or embark on an affair for the sake of the material rewards.

ten of pentacles

Upright
An established secure home, family or relationship. This card can also indicate the actual fabric of a home, which is usually an older property in pleasant surroundings, where several generations of the family have lived.

Reversed
This card indicates disharmony in a usually secure, established home, such as petty quarrels and potential disorganization. There could also be instability regarding the family and finances.

page of pentacles

Upright
News about security is coming your way. This may be a win of money, a birthday gift or a small inheritance. It may be that you hear of a job vacancy, and you get the job.

Reversed
This card indicates that a person younger than yourself is giving you news or information in relation to security.

knight of pentacles

Upright
This person is determined to get ahead in life. They plan strategically, knowing exactly how to succeed. This is a focused person.

Reversed
Similar to the upright Knight, but ruthless. These types will tend to burn their bridges as they continue to move up in the world, thereby making plenty of enemies along the way.

queen of pentacles

Upright
This card indicates a woman with strong maternal and material instincts. Her domestic life is important to her, and marriage and children are the path she often chooses. She will work hard to make her surroundings comfortable.

Reversed
This woman goes ruthlessly towards her goals. Often this reflects a very insecure or unstable childhood. She overcompensates for security and love by chasing financial success.

king of pentacles

Upright
A successful and powerful man with a great sense of responsibility towards his family, friends and career. He does not come across as overconfident. Usually he will make a sympathetic and caring partner for a woman.

Reversed
When reversed, this King is very insecure about his role. This may be due to a failed marriage, business or lack of interest from his children. He finds it hard to let go of the past.

minor arcana: cups

When the suit of Cups is present in a reading, the issues are connected with love, emotions and intuitive faculties. The symbol of the cup resembles a chalice or sacred drinking vessel and brings to mind the holy grail or the cup of life. Consequently, the issues of the Cups cards have a spiritual quality. The suit of Cups is related to the element of water. It equates to the suit of Hearts in the pack of playing cards.

ace of cups

Upright
This card is also known as the "Holy Grail" or "Cup of Life". Some consider it to be by far the most important card. It indicates a miracle or blessing. Any subject that the Ace of Cups is near will be blessed with good fortune.

Reversed
This card denotes disappointment or sadness. It can indicate a person with a large ego. This person tends to fall quite hard and they need to accept other people's views and feelings.

two of cups

Upright
This card represents the forming of an important relationship built on common interests, friendship and a higher understanding of adult love and companionship. Usually it will be sustainable over a long period of time and grow and develop.

Reversed
A disagreement has taken place between two parties that is really quite petty. One person needs to break the ice and make the important first move towards reconciliation.

three of cups

Upright
This card denotes rejoicing, optimism and growth. It indicates formal celebrations of events such as weddings, anniversaries, christenings, or a promotion.

Reversed
Formal celebrations of happy events will meet with some discord. This may arise through personality conflicts, or bad timing in communications when things would have been better dealt with at another time in another place.

four of cups

Upright
This card indicates a new friendship. It can also warn that an offer of an emotional nature will be put to you, but with strings attached. It would be wise to find out what these strings are before accepting the offer.

Reversed
You may be the victim of feeling that "the grass is greener on the other side" and have now got yourself emotionally involved in a situation that is not as good as it first seemed.

five of cups

Upright
You are in a situation in which an emotional sacrifice will need to be made, such as deciding between your husband and children, and your lover. In this case the lover would be sacrificed because of the commitment to your family.

Reversed
A similar type of sacrifice would have to be made as in the upright card, but in this instance it is less heart-rending. For example, it might be between your hobby and your career.

six of cups

Upright
This card shows that you are currently dealing with memories of your past. These may be connected with a person, with issues that were important in your childhood, or they may be concerned with children themselves.

Reversed
The reversed card indicates memories from the recent past. You will be dealing with a memory of a person or an event from roughly within the last five years.

seven of cups

Upright
This card indicates that you have plenty of opportunities and may be unsure of which one to choose. Whichever one you take will prove very rewarding and emotionally fulfilling.

Reversed
Emotionally it seems that there is no one interesting or nothing that fascinates you. This barren time will quickly pass.

eight of cups

Upright
All that has been familiar to you emotionally, such as a secure relationship, has now gone past its "sell-by date". It may be time to venture out into the world alone.

Reversed
You are able to re-evaluate yourself and the past. This enables you to abandon old ties and move forwards to the future.

nine of cups

Upright
You are feeling a sense of emotional abundance, sensuality and fulfilment, and that "all is right with the world".

Reversed
This card denotes complacency. Emotionally you are quite spoilt, and you may be in danger of taking for granted the love and attention you receive from others with whom you have relationships. There may also be the feeling that you are never satisfied with your life.

ten of cups

Upright
This card represents a fresh, new start in the home. This can be an actual new home, or introducing a new aspect to the existing one – such as a child, a new partner, or even making structural changes to the property.

Reversed
You will experience stress on the domestic front due to a disruption or a new introduction into the home. These stresses will usually work themselves through given some time and patience.

page of cups

Upright
This card is always present when a person is trying to gain your affection or attention. It is known as the "Courtship Card".

Reversed
The reversed card is similar to the upright definition, except that the attention will come from a person younger than yourself.

knight of cups

Upright
The Knight of Cups can indicate a lover or a more abstract affair of the heart such as artistic self-expression. Perhaps a new partner is putting on their best behaviour to court you.

Reversed
This card denotes a person will be flirtatious, wanting affection due to their own lack of self-worth.

queen of cups

Upright
This woman has an ability to listen to others and to be interested in what they have to say. She is captivating and has a sensual, understated look that attracts others. The Queen of Cups makes a wonderful partner, friend, mother and colleague.

Reversed
Similar to the upright Queen, but plagued by deeply-rooted insecurity, doubting herself. This means that she may stay in relationships where her good nature is taken for granted.

king of cups

Upright
This man likes people. He enjoys socializing and entertaining and is at his best when he has an appreciative audience. He is creative and is drawn to the world of art, theatre and music.

Reversed
This man suffers from deep insecurities and has a tendency to get involved with people who are not good for him. Owing to his need to be noticed, he will go to great lengths to get attention. He needs to watch out for depression.

reading the tarot

The Tarot is a user-friendly form of divination because of the highly visual prompt that each of the 78 cards contains. For thousands of years, people have communicated through the use of creative thought and story-telling. By learning to interpret the Tarot with discretion and kindness for your friends and family, you can continue this age-old practice of learning from the spoken word and picture.

Almost as much energy needs to be put in before interpreting the Tarot cards as into the actual reading itself. It is important to create a calm environment, preferably with soft lighting, as the setting for a reading. Too much background noise or too many bright lights can disturb your concentration. Privacy is also vitally important because quite personal and adult subjects may be discussed while doing a reading for another person (who is known as the "querent"). Eye contact and a caring smile always help the querent to feel at ease when you are reading their cards.

At the beginning of the reading, the querent should concentrate on the subject or issue of their reading. At the same time, they should handle the cards, shuffling them in some way. As soon as the querent feels they have concentrated and handled the cards for long enough, they can stop. This process will be different for each individual. Some people will take only a short time to get issues clear in their minds, while others will take longer to focus. However, it must be left up to the querent to decide when they are ready. They should pass you the deck when they finish. It is during the shuffling process that some of the cards become reversed. This is caused by the querent either deliberately turning the cards around, or by dropping a few in the handling process and putting them back in the deck reversed. Either way, it is the individual's unique handling of the cards that will determine how they fall when they are passed over to you to be interpreted.

When you finish a reading, always ask the querent if they understand and accept the information you have given them. It is with this final step that you will be able to monitor your skill as a reader, and gradually increase your skill in reading the cards effectively. For instance, perhaps everything that you said was true – then great! That will give you a real boost of confidence. Or maybe some things were incorrect – the person will let you know either way. Even if the whole reading was incorrect, you should not let this put you off, but remember that you are still learning and we all learn through our mistakes.

how to read the tarot

When you are giving or receiving a reading, the best way to look at this beautiful deck of cards is that it is like going to a good friend for advice. Remember that it does not control fate, or tell you how to live your life: but it can raise issues and help to give you a clearer picture of where you stand. If you are just starting to practise reading the Tarot, let the querent know that you are a beginner.

1 Gently clear and focus your mind. Try to let go of your own personal problems or issues. This will get easier with time, although if you have difficulty doing this now, try focusing your mind on one thing, such as a rainbow or a sunrise.

2 Clear the pack of cards by making sure all the cards are upright before giving them to the querent. To give the querent reversed cards is unfair, as their reading would be influenced by the actions of the previous person who handled the cards.

3 Next, shuffle the cards. It is vital to do this as it gives the cards a fresh start. The tarot cards are larger than normal playing cards and this may take practice. Make sure you focus on keeping your mind clear while doing this.

4 Ask the querent to concentrate as clearly as possible on the issues or areas of life that she is currently concerned about and that she wishes the cards to comment on. These will be the ones you will be interpreting for her.

5 Hand the querent the pack of cards and ask her to shuffle it. She should still be concentrating on the issues she wants the Tarot to look into. Only when she feels that she has shuffled the cards for long enough should she hand the complete pack back to you.

6 Choose whichever spread you are most comfortable with, draw the cards from the top of the pack and lay them down in the correct sequence, face up. As you gain more practice, you will learn other sequences, which may be more or less complicated, and adapt them to your reading.

7 Now read the cards. Remember that you are starting to learn and understand the Tarot. If what you are interpreting does not make sense or is too delicate a subject to take up, it is best to use discretion and plead ignorance in order to take the pressure off.

8 When you have ascertained and interpreted all you can from the cards, let the querent know that you have finished the reading by drawing to a conclusion. Ask if she has understood and accepted the information you have given her.

quick guides

This one-page guide to the meanings of the Tarot cards may be useful while you are learning to interpret them. The brief notes on the Major Arcana will help you to remember their meanings in general terms. For the cards of the Minor Arcana, take the general background definition of the particular suit and cross-reference it with the general numerical meaning for the number given below.

MAJOR ARCANA

FOOL — Spontaneity, change, risk
MAGICIAN — Preparation, flexibility
HIGH PRIESTESS — Intuition, premonition
EMPRESS — Fertility, domestic bliss
EMPEROR — Organization, authority
HIEROPHANT — Professional advice, ritual
LOVERS — Instant chemistry

CHARIOT — Competition, victory
JUSTICE — Fairness, balance
HERMIT — Self-awareness, renewal
WHEEL OF FORTUNE — Fate, redirection
STRENGTH — Fortitude, self-belief
HANGED MAN — Stagnation, renewal
DEATH — Regeneration, transformation
TEMPERANCE — Circumspection, self-control

DEVIL — New passion, energy
TOWER — Disruption of past ties
STAR — Wish come true
MOON — Deception, insincerity
SUN — Progress, growth
JUDGEMENT — Lifting of restriction
WORLD — Success, contentment

MINOR ARCANA

ACE — Potential, new, beginnings
TWO — Affirmation, choice, pledge, commitment
THREE — Clarification, plans made public, appreciation
FOUR — Manifestion, creation of a plan, stoicism
FIVE — Adjustment, challenge, possible conflict
SIX — Poise, contentment, victory
SEVEN — Imagination, options, variety

EIGHT — Organization, evaluation, experience, commitments
NINE — Integration, contentment
TEN — Hesitation, resistance to change
PAGE — Information
KNIGHT — Focus, single-minded
QUEEN — Fulfilment, deep satisfaction, skill, maturity
KING — Competition, realization

the celtic cross spread

The Celtic Cross is the best Tarot spread to use when you have a specific question on your mind that can be answered with a "yes" or "no", such as "I have just had a job interview – will I get the job?" This is because it deals with one issue at a time. Lay the cards out following the order of the sequence shown. The position of each card refers to a different issue as listed below.

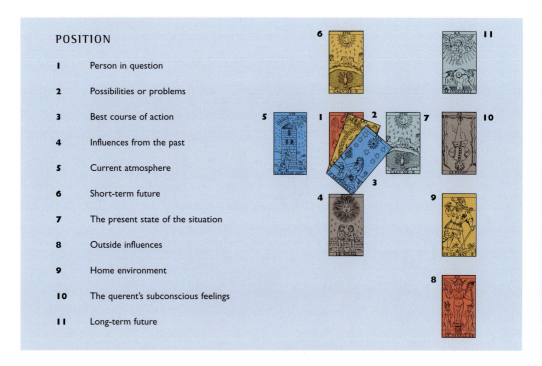

POSITION	
1	Person in question
2	Possibilities or problems
3	Best course of action
4	Influences from the past
5	Current atmosphere
6	Short-term future
7	The present state of the situation
8	Outside influences
9	Home environment
10	The querent's subconscious feelings
11	Long-term future

THE CELTIC CROSS EXPLAINED

1 Person in question: The card in this position indicates the querent.

2 Possibilities or problems: This will indicate either possibilities for a solution and a positive way forwards, or problems that may occur along the way.

3 Best course of action: This shows the road to follow in order to achieve the desired outcome.

4 Influences from the past: This card is about a person or something from the querent's past that is present now or affecting the current situation.

5 Current atmosphere: This represents the mood of the situation. This may be light and positive or heavy and serious.

6 Short-term future: This represents how the situation will develop over the next three months.

7 The present state of the situation: This tells us whether the current situation is precarious or stable. It indicates where it is now in relation to the future outcome.

8 Outside influences: This represents other people or issues that may have an effect on the desired outcome or that need to be taken into consideration.

9 Home environment: This tells us something about the querent's home environment at the present time.

10 The querent's subconscious feelings: This indicates whether the querent feels positive or negative about the situation and its outcome.

11 Long-term future: The final card of the spread represents the likely long-term outcome of the situation, forecasting over the next six to twelve months.

SAMPLE READING

1 Person in question: Death: This woman has formulated a whole new outlook on her life, and has recently discovered new energy, both mentally and physically.

2 Possibilities or problems: Five of Swords: She may feel the need to prove herself morally in the right over the issue that is concerning her, or to show that she is correct to have her new energetic feelings.

3 Best course of action: The Hermit: Now she should take "time out" for herself so she can gather all her thoughts and feelings towards her new-found direction.

4 Influences from the past: King of Cups: A very people-oriented man associated with the recent past might be the cause for her new thoughts, feelings and inspiration.

5 Current atmosphere: Two of Pentacles: Now it may be best to carry on juggling two important aspects of her life in order to keep things in balance for the moment.

6 Short-term future: Eight of Cups: Over the next three months, this woman will be making an emotional departure from her old lifestyle and going in a new direction.

7 The present state of the situation: Page of Cups: She will be very popular and sought after as she moves in her new direction.

8 Outside influences: Four of Swords: It would be best to keep her thoughts or opinions about her future direction, right or wrong, to herself. This is so that she can maintain some sort of control over her thoughts about her new direction.

9 Home environment: Six of Cups: The woman is looking at the home she lives in at the moment as a past-tense situation. A new home is likely in the near future.

10 The querent's subconscious feelings: The Hanged Man: Subconsciously she feels that she is in a rut, and she is looking forward to making even bigger changes in her life when the time is right.

11 Long-term future: The High Priestess: The woman is right to put her trust in her instincts and gut feelings about her life. It is by following her intuition that she has been able to make the choices that she is now acting upon.

the romany spread

In the past, this spread was used most widely by travelling fortune-tellers. It is also known as the Gypsy spread. Many Tarot readers find it useful because it can look at a person's past, present and future together. It is best used when the querent has various issues that they are dealing with and they want to see how these things will turn out. The querent is simply seeking some general insights into their current situation.

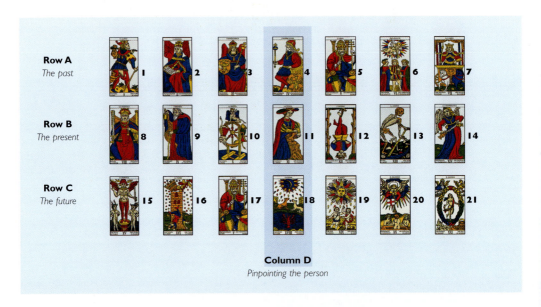

Column D
Pinpointing the person

THE ROMANY SPREAD EXPLAINED

ROW A The Past
The first set of seven cards deals with the querent's past. Cards 1, 2 and 3 represent the more distant past, while cards 5, 6 and 7 represent the more recent past.

ROW B The Present
The second set of seven cards engages with present-time issues that are going on for the querent. "What is going on right now?"

ROW C The Future
The final set of seven cards looks to the future of a person's life and what is likely to take place in this time. The future is taken to mean the span of time over the next eight months.

COLUMN D Pinpointing the Person
Cards 4, 11 and 18 form a central vertical column. By interpreting this small group of three cards, the reader can gain an insight into what the querent is really curious or concerned about.

Reading the Cards

The Romany spread consists of three rows of seven cards. These three rows correspond to the past, present and future. The middle card of each row is also read as a separate vertical column, and relates to the querent. Begin reading with Column D, then read the rows A, B, and C from left to right.

SAMPLE READING FOR A MAN

Column D: By looking first at column D (cards in positions 4, 11 and 18) you can deduce that this man is feeling emotionally balanced with a positive and focused attitude. There is also a nurturing and caring woman in his life.

Row A: In the past, some information about a financial issue (possibly his career) led this man in a new direction, moving away from his past associations. This direction, which gave him a great feeling of excitement, turned into his way of life. Now, however, he needs to put his trust in a new direction.

Row B: As the querent has balance in his home life, he can take on new routines and improve his present situation. This can be best accomplished by being careful with finances and staying well-organized.

Row C: A blessing in disguise will take place for this man, but it means that a three-way emotional involvement will not work out. He should focus on the friendship of the strong, nurturing female in his life. By doing so, his creative endeavours will bear fruit.

Column D
Pinpointing the person

SAMPLE READING FOR A WOMAN

Column D: By looking first at column D (cards in positions 4, 11 and 18), you deduce that this woman has specific goals relating to her career. She is looking for more money and greater opportunities to support her interests.

Row A : This woman has high moral standards and was stressed in the past due to her sense of fair play. Recently, she has embarked on a particular professional goal by taking new steps and a calculated risk at her own expense, leaving her feeling a bit isolated, like the Hermit.

Row B: The woman is seeking professional advice about her situation, as she feels betrayed professionally by something that has jeopardized her plans. She seems to have the support of a philosophical partner, who encourages her to make positive choices.

Row C: She will soon receive news about a professional goal which will leave her feeling more emotionally balanced. The final outcome is one of total success in all areas of her life.

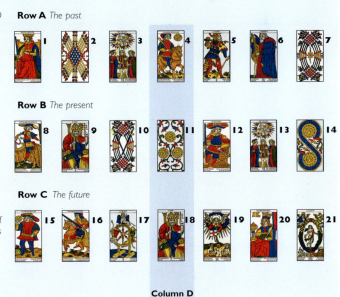

Column D
Pinpointing the person

I Ching

People have always sought answers to what might be. Will I be wealthy? Will I achieve my goal? Will I marry? Will I be happy? It seems to be an intrinsic part of human nature to want to know what the future holds. This is understandable: the future can be a frightening proposition, but there are no absolutes. Paradoxically, the only certainty in life is change: things are always in a state of flux, day slips into night and night into day. Inorganic elements are transmuted into organic life that progresses through a series of changes, and when that life ends the elements are released and another change is initiated. Spring progresses to summer, summer to autumn, autumn to winter and winter to spring.

In all change, however, there are certain patterns, and it is this predictability that the shamans of ancient China referred to when they were called upon to give advice and divinations on forthcoming events. These "bamboo shamans" of 4,000 years ago burnt the shoulder blade of an ox, inscribed with the particular question, and divined the answer from the patterns of the cracks that appeared. Later they used tortoise shells in the same manner, the tortoise being revered as a symbol of wisdom and longevity.

This was the origin of the I Ching, which translates as "The Book of Changes". As it developed, it became more than just an oracular device for fortune-telling. The ancient sages began to see that this body of wisdom could be used as a blueprint for understanding the workings of the universe.

the origins of the i ching

The I Ching has survived invasions, wars and other tumultuous cultural upheavals. It was first devised from observing the natural world, the ebb and flow of its cycles. The counsel the I Ching offers is based upon adopting a more harmonious approach to life, having an awareness and a respect for the influences acting upon every part of the universe, including humanity.

Yin and Yang

According to ancient Chinese philosophy, the time before the universe and the earth were created was known as Wu Chi, which means "ultimate nothingness". Out of this formless chaos was born the principle of yin and yang, the fundamental law underlying all of creation. Yin and yang are represented by the Tai Chi, the well-known symbol comprised of a circle divided into two equal segments, one black, one white. These are the complementary opposites apparent in everything; one cannot exist without the other, although they are characterized by extremities that make them seem poles apart. Where yin is dark, yang is light; where yin is weak, yang is firm; where yin is feminine, yang is masculine; where yin is receptive, yang is active, and so on.

Yin and yang lines can be combined in pairs to give four different variations.

The Unifying Principle

The Tai Chi symbolizes the polarity of the two forces but it also shows a germinative quality: each holds within itself the seed of the other, and each is in constant flux: yang starts from a small point, grows and at its peak transforms into yin, which starts from a small point, transmuting to yang at its zenith, and so the cycle continues. Yin and yang are transient states of being, and the interplay of these two elemental energies, or forces, gives rise to creation. A good example is a pan of boiling water. As heat is applied and it begins to simmer, the water near the bottom expands and rises, exhibiting yang qualities; this allows the cooler water, the yin component, to sink. The polarity has now been reversed and what was yin becomes yang, and vice versa.

The Pa Kua

Both the trigrams and the hexagrams of the I Ching are known as *kua*, and the customary arrangement of the eight trigrams (*pa kua*) is often used together with the Tai Chi as a charm or talisman to ward off harm. The Pa Kua appears on flags and plaques, and around geomantic mirrors. Two layouts are used: the Early Heaven Arrangement, attributed to the legendary emperor Fu Hsi, and the Later Heaven Arrangement, shown here, which is attributed to Wen, first emperor of the Chou dynasty, who expanded and refined the I Ching by creating the 64 hexagrams.

YIN	YANG
Moon	Sun
Winter	Summer
Dark	Light
Feminine	Masculine
Interior	Exterior
Low	High
Stillness	Movement
Silence	Noise
Passive	Active
Odd numbers	Even numbers
Earth	Heaven
Shade	Sunshine
Cold	Heat
Soft	Hard
Valleys	Hills
Still water	Mountains
Gardens	Houses
Sleep	Wakefulness

Gradations of Yin and Yang

It is not known how long ago the philosophy of yin and yang first appeared in written form but the symbols have been in use for millennia. Yang is represented by a single unbroken line and yin by a single broken line:

⎯⎯⎯⎯ yang (positive)
⎯ ⎯ yin (negative)

In this basic form, these symbols can be used in a simple "yes/no" fashion and a question can be answered with the toss of a coin. Yang is "yes", the "heads" side of the coin and yin is "no", the "tails" side. However, this system gives no depth or insight into the nature of a situation, no gradation showing what areas can change to give a satisfactory outcome.

Yin and yang are very definite – black and white, hard and soft, and so on – and there are an infinite number of points between the two extremes. This polarity of opposites was only the beginning of a philosophical system that could be used to study the workings of the universe and to apply it to aligning humans with the creative principle. There are also relative values of yin and yang: a person or thing can be yang in relation to A but yin in relation to B. For example, water is yang compared to wind but yin compared to wood, while wood is yang compared to water but yin compared to rock. Rock is yang when compared to wood but yin in comparison with fire.

Creation results from a synergy of the two forces working together and combining to form different structures. The ancient Chinese sages realized that to give a more tonal quality, to produce the gradation or "shading", further refinement was necessary. To this end, a second line was added to each yin or yang line. The pairs could be combined to produce four different variations which could be used to represent intermediate states of being: yang-yang is yang at its fullest; yin-yin is yin at its fullest; yang-yin is "rising" yang; and yin-yang is "rising" yin.

The Cardinal Directions

These four new symbols gave different strengths to the two basic ones. They were seen to fit with the natural order of the world, and each was associated with one of the four cardinal directions. In this way they came to be arrayed in a square form. They were also seen to be representative of the four seasons and times of day, and the gradation was thus perceived to progress in a natural and symmetrical way.

Yang-yin was aligned with the east, the spring and the sunrise; yang-yang, with the positive energy at its fullest, with the south, the summer and with noon, the brightest time of the day. Yin-yang was associated with the west, the autumn and the sunset, and yin-yin with the north, the winter, and with midnight.

The Pa Kua

Further refinement came with the addition of a third line to produce the eight basic trigrams which came to form the basis of the I Ching. The eight symbols were given specific names and arranged in the Pa Kua, an eight-sided figure derived from the previous square form, showing the opposing pairs of forces. The Tai Chi symbol of yin and yang frequently appears in the centre of the diagram. The trigrams are read from the bottom upwards or from the centre of the Pa Kua outwards.

The venerated sage and philosopher, Confucius, who valued the I Ching highly and extended its use and popularity.

development of the I Ching

The I Ching, itself very ancient, was the crystallization in written form of an even older tradition of divination, in which the patterns seen in nature were used as indicators of the likely outcome of immediate conditions. These patterns were formalized in the symbols of the I Ching, with commentaries to interpret the patterns and offer insights into the forces, or changes, occurring at a given time.

A Blueprint for the Universe

The early stages of the I Ching are shrouded in ancient myth and legend, but the original rendition of the work into written form is credited to the legendary first Emperor of China, Fu Hsi. Fu Hsi was said to have been a great sage and scholar. He was also credited with the invention of weaving and the making of fishing nets, and was seen as a great benefactor of his people. After many years observing and contemplating the natural world and himself, he came to an understanding of the basic patterns underlying everything. Using this wisdom, he composed the eight three-lined diagrams (the trigrams) which are the basis of the I Ching. According to one legend, the emperor saw the trigrams in the patterns on the back of a tortoise. The story relates to the tradition of using tortoise shells in divination by heating them in a fire until they cracked, then interpreting the patterns of the cracks. The eight trigrams represented the eight fundamental forces of nature which embody and exemplify the creation that surrounds us.

The original Pa Kua was called the "Early Heaven Arrangement" but it was revised at a later date to give a clearer definition of the dynamic interplay of the complementary opposites which work together to produce the changes in creation.

A portrait of the legendary first Emperor, the learned Fu Hsi.

The Development of the Trigrams

During the next millennium the trigrams were largely untouched, the next transformation being attributed to King Wen, a feudal lord from the province of Chou in western China. According to tradition, King Wen was imprisoned in 1143 BC by the Emperor Chou Hsin.

While he languished in prison, King Wen passed the time by working with the trigrams. He found that by arranging them in all possible paired combinations they produced 64 six-lined diagrams (hexagrams). He also wrote a commentary on the hexagrams that refined the interplay of the energies that each of them symbolized, explaining them and giving advice on what needed to be looked at in relation to the question that had been asked during a consultation. After his release from prison, King Wen waged war against Chou Hsin, eventually overthrowing him and founding the Chou dynasty.

King Wen's son, the Duke of Chou, added another dimension to the 64 hexagrams of the I Ching by giving each line a specific meaning for a deeper insight. The individual lines are highlighted by transforming yin and yang, when each force at its extreme is changed to its opposite.

Later History of the I Ching

Some 500 years later the venerable Chinese sage and philosopher Confucius, who valued the I Ching highly, added more observations and commentaries to the treatise. This gave further weight to an already significant work and extended its popularity as an oracle to be consulted in order to determine a course of action to effect a beneficial change in a situation. In AD 175, the texts of the "Five Confucian Classics", including the I Ching, were engraved on stone.

The I Ching became an integral part of Chinese culture, but did not become widely known in the West until it was translated in the late 19th century by the German missionary and Sinologist, Richard Wilhelm. This initial translation into German was readily embraced by the renowned psychiatrist Carl Jung, who saw it as confirmation of his theories of synchronicity and the subconscious. An English translation soon followed and numerous other translations and interpretations have ensured its widespread appeal, giving people from all walks of life advice on problems and self-development.

A carved stone tortoise, symbolizing wisdom, commemorates the story of the beginnings of the I Ching.

the eight trigrams

The trigrams were given attributes and characteristics that helped to define them symbolically in terms of the natural world, human social arrangements, colours, animal totems and body parts, to name just a few. In an I Ching consultation, these images are used metaphorically to give depth and refinement to the hexagrams that are constructed by arranging the trigrams in pairs.

 Ch'ien represents heaven, the power of the universe, and the creative. In the family it is the father, and in the body it is associated with the head. It is strong and active, the three yang lines representing vitality, limitless potential and endurance. Its colour is blinding white and its animal is the horse. It also symbolizes ice and the fruit of a tree.

 K'an represents water, the abysmal. In the family it is the middle son, and the body part is the ear. It is dangerous and fearless, full of hidden perils and swirling, erosive forces. Its colour is deep blue and its animal the pig or boar. It is also symbolic of marrowy wood, soft and spongy, able to soak up water but lacking great strength.

 K'un represents earth, the receptive. The family member is the mother and the body part is the belly. It is gentle and passive, the three yin lines representing endless nurturing and devotion. Its colour is black and its animal is the cow. It also symbolizes the supportive tree trunk and a large cloth or cart, carrying all things without distinction.

Li represents fire, the clinging. In the family it is the middle daughter, and in the body the eyes. It is bright, warm and clear, corresponding to beauty and intelligence. The lives of others benefit from its radiance. Its colour is warm orange, the colour of fire and the sun, and its animal is the peacock. Li also represents dry, brittle trees.

 Chen represents thunder, the arousing. In the family it is the eldest son, and in the body it is the foot. It is violent and determined, filled with spontaneity and excitement. Its colour is bright red and its animal is the dragon, the symbol of speed and power. It also represents the fast-growing reed, volcanoes and earthquakes.

Ken represents the mountain, the stillness. The family member is the youngest son and the body part is the hand. It is calm, meditative and earnest, able to withdraw yet to grasp things firmly. Its colour is imperial purple and its animal is the dog. It is also seen as a hermit and as a strong, gnarled tree, twisted from its position on a mountain.

 Sun represents wind, the gentle and penetrating. In the family it is the eldest daughter, and in the body the thighs. It is soothing yet persevering and just, characterizing flexibility and strength, and permeating all things like the wind. Its colour is lush green and its animal is the cat or tiger. It also symbolizes tall, graceful trees such as the willow, that can bend before the wind and spring back easily.

 Tui represents the lake, the joyful. In the family it is the youngest daughter, and in the body it is associated with the mouth and lips, always ready to smile in friendliness. It is tender and sensual on the outside, making it attractive and inviting, yet it possesses a hard, iron core. Its colour is yellow and its animal is the sheep. It also evokes the spirit of a witch or sorceress, and represents mist and harvests.

consulting the oracle

The I Ching does not tell you what to do. It counsels on the nature of a problem and the best way to deal with it. It is the Sage that is aware of all possibilities and the insights it offers are pertinent to you and your situation. The onus of effecting the change is on you accepting the advice and acting on it. For a consultation several things are needed, physical and metaphysical, but principally a reflective state of mind.

Ritual

The most important factors to bring to an I Ching consultation are an open mind and humility. It is not necessary to prostrate yourself, but you do need to leave your ego at the door to show proper respect to a wise and venerated Sage. In fact, the humility has already begun because you have taken the first steps in approaching the oracle for advice, recognizing that you have a need for assistance and that there is a higher power you can call upon.

As an aid to achieving a calm and receptive state of mind when approaching the I Ching, it is useful to perform a small ritual to help you relax and focus your intent. Light a candle and contemplate the flame. A living flame is beautiful and as you give it your attention imagine it illuminating you inside. Burn some incense: its calming effects have been used for thousands of years and the smoke also has cleans-

Hold the coins for a moment in your hand before you throw them, as you would throw dice.

ing properties. As you watch the smoke, imagine it pervading your aura, purifying it of any negative energies that you have accumulated. Pass the coins through the incense smoke to purify them. The effects of the smoke will also cleanse the auras of objects and places. Breathe deeply and slowly from your diaphragm for a few breaths. This helps to relax you and focus your attention.

When consulting the I Ching you are circumventing the conscious mind, and all the hormones and emotions that have such a large effect on it, and contacting the higher self. This is the part of you which is in direct communication with the rest of creation, the part of you through which intuition flows and which wants only what is best for you. With time and practice it will become easier to reach a calm state of mind and it may be that after a while a ritual is unnecessary, although it does serve to differentiate the consultation from the day-to-day life you are seeking help with.

Formulating a Question

What are you consulting the I Ching about? What are you seeking guidance on? It is necessary to determine the subject first so that you can pose the question in a way that is not at all ambiguous. It is necessary to approach the subject with the seriousness it deserves. The I Ching is not a party game and will not respond if you ask frivolous questions or are indifferent to the counsel it offers.

Some people consult the I Ching on a daily basis concerning the best way to act on that day, others consult it only at times of crisis or when at a crossroads in life. The frequency is not important, but if you ask too often it is a sign that you are probably not relaxed. Don't repeat questions because that indicates that you have no faith in the answer you first received; this may lead to the Sage withdrawing assistance and further answers you receive will be confused or garbled.

Try to maintain an objective, detached attitude. If you are emotionally involved in the question, if it is of great importance to you when you ask it, the charged nature of your physical state will interfere with the clarity of the process. In an emotional state you will also be less receptive to the answer you receive because it may not be the one you were hoping for.

Write your question down to clarify it and help you focus on it.

Constructing a Hexagram

The usual way to construct a hexagram is to cast three coins. They can be of any denomination but it is best if they are all of the same size and value. Old Chinese coins are satisfying to use.

Use the same coins each time and do not let anyone else touch them because their auras can be influenced by energies from another source. Treat them with respect because they are an important link to the Sage. Traditionally the coins were blessed and purified then stored with the I Ching on a shelf above shoulder height, only to be moved for purposes of a consultation.

The faces of the coins are assigned a value, which when added together determines whether a line of a hexagram will be yin or yang. The "heads" side (the more heavily inscribed side on a Chinese coin) is considered yang and is valued at three, while the "tails" side is yin and is given a value of two. When the coins are thrown, a total of six, seven, eight or nine is obtained, giving lines that are either yin (even numbers) or yang (odd numbers).

Hold the coins while you focus on what you seek guidance on, then shake them gently in your cupped hands while concentrating on the question. Drop the coins on to a hard surface such as a table or the floor and add up their values. Repeat five times until you have six totals. The first line is at the bottom and the hexagram is constructed upwards, following the path of organic growth. In the following example, x denotes "heads" (3) and – denotes "tails" (2):

```
Sixth throw:    x  x  –  = 8
Fifth throw:    x  x  –  = 8      K'un    ==
Fourth throw:   x  x  –  = 8

Third throw:    x  –  –  = 7
Second throw:   x  –  –  = 7      Ch'ien  ≡
First throw:    x  –  –  = 7
```

If, when you cast the coins, you throw only sevens and eights it indicates that the answer is very clear and you need only read the interpretation of the relevant hexagram.

Old Chinese coins have a symbolic connection with the I Ching.

Use candles to help you in your meditation while you are concentrating on the situation you wish to ask a question about.

Changing Lines

The totals of the coins' faces can produce two odd numbers and two even numbers. The seven and the eight stay the same. The six and the nine, however, represent old yin and old yang which means that they are at their extremes, so each changes to its opposite, altering the result and giving you a second hexagram to interpret as part of the consultation.

Six is old yin, written —x— and becomes young yang.
Seven is young yang, written ——— and stays the same.
Eight is young yin, written — — and stays the same.
Nine is old yang, written —•— and changes to young yin.

The changing lines give deeper insights into a reading. The initial hexagram relates to present conditions; the changing lines produce a second hexagram which relates to the future outcome of a situation or helps to clarify the original question. If you receive a hexagram with changing lines, read the interpretation of the first hexagram and the lines that are changing, then go to the second hexagram and read the interpretation only. The following example shows changing lines:

```
Sixth throw:    x  x  x  = 9
Fifth throw:    x  –  –  = 7     Sun becomes K'an
Fourth throw:   x  x  –  = 8

Third throw:    x  x  –  = 8
Second throw:   –  –  –  = 6     Chen becomes Tui
First throw:    x  –  –  = 7
```

The first throw produced hexagram number 42, I (Increase), with lines two and six changing, which then gave hexagram number 60, Chieh (Limitation). Going to the relevant entry, you would read the interpretation and lines two and six of I, then you would go to Chieh and read the interpretation only.

table of trigrams

Once the hexagram is obtained, it can be identified using this table. The left-hand side shows the lower trigrams, and the top shows the upper trigrams. Find the component trigrams of the hexagram you have constructed and the square where they meet will give the number of the hexagram. When you have that number, turn to the relevant entry and read the interpretation of it.

Lower Trigrams \ Upper Trigrams	CH'IEN	CHEN	K'AN	KEN	TUI	LI	SUN	K'UN
CH'IEN	1	34	5	26	43	14	9	11
CHEN	25	51	3	27	17	21	42	24
K'AN	6	40	29	4	47	64	59	7
KEN	33	62	39	52	31	56	53	15
TUI	10	54	60	41	58	38	61	19
LI	13	55	63	22	49	30	37	36
SUN	44	32	48	18	28	50	57	46
K'UN	12	16	8	23	45	35	20	2

table of hexagrams

This table shows the 64 hexagrams, arranged according to the trigrams which make them up. Hexagrams are always constructed from the bottom up, which is also the traditional method of writing Chinese characters. This follows the patterns and structures of nature, since everything grows from the ground upwards. Like the trigrams, each hexagram has a name and a basic meaning.

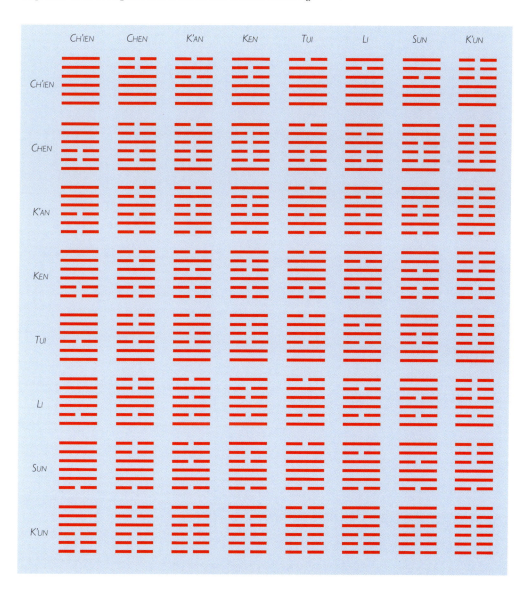

the hexagrams

The 64 hexagrams of the I Ching are all the possible combinations of the eight trigrams of the Pa Kua. Although two trigrams form a complete hexagram, they maintain their individuality in the structure by virtue of their relative positions. The lower trigram represents the basis or foundation of the situation, and the upper trigram reflects the manner in which the circumstances can unfold or develop. In addition to this distinction, each of the six lines has its own significance in terms of its position in the hexagram, which is read from the bottom upwards.

The first line (at the bottom) is related to the early beginnings of a situation and can be seen as someone of low social standing. The second line is where the subject resides: this is the core of the lower trigram. The third line is the transition from the lower trigram to the upper and is associated with the pitfalls that lie in wait for someone rising above their station without due care.

The fourth line is seen as the officer, the intermediary between the ruler and the masses. As the first line of the upper trigram it also signifies a successful rise from the lower trigram to the upper.

The fifth line represents the ruler, and is the core of the upper trigram. It can also symbolize good fortune. The sixth line indicates that there are things beyond even rulers and is a caution against reaching too high.

The commentaries on the 64 hexagrams are set out on the following pages, with the Duke of Chou's additional observations, which should be read for changing lines. If you receive a hexagram with changing lines, read the interpretation of the first hexagram and the lines that are changing, then go to the second hexagram produced by the changing lines and read the interpretation only.

To benefit from reading the interpretation you need to keep the same open, detached frame of mind with which you formulated your question and constructed the hexagram. Read the text carefully. It may be useful to note down your immediate responses or thoughts relating to the interpretation. If you feel that the answers you have received are unclear, it could mean that you did not phrase your question with sufficient clarity, or that you are not in a sufficiently receptive state on this occasion. Leave it and come back to it later.

乾 1 CH'IEN – The creative *Masculine, dynamic, inspiring, overbearing*

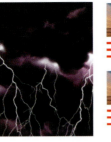
Heaven

Heaven

Heaven over heaven represents the ceaseless creative force that is available if you follow the proper principles. If you are true to yourself and release old habits, you will allow the superior qualities of humility, patience, acceptance and tolerance to grow. Be strong and true and the energy of creation will flow through you, unfolding your destiny and leading to great things. Trust that the unknowable workings of fate serve only to help you grow stronger, and retain your inner truth.

Line readings

6 Retain your humility and acceptance, or you will suffer a great fall.
5 Join with other like-minded people and work together for mutual benefit.
4 Trust in your inner truth to guide you and do not hesitate in coming to a decision when you have to make a choice.
3 Do not let adulation go to your head.
2 The best way to exert an influence is to lead by example.
1 Be patient and listen to your heart to tell you when to act.

坤 2 K'UN – The receptive *Feminine, yielding, gentle, providing, bountiful*

Earth

Earth

This is the complement to the first hexagram. For the creative to take root and flourish, it needs receptive ground to provide nourishment. Cultivate the receptive nature that will provide the appropriate ground for wisdom to grow. The earth is the endless provider, giving without seeking recognition. This is the time to follow because there is not enough experience to lead or initiate change. Concentrate on developing inner strength: what you receive now will produce bountiful results in future.

Line readings

6 Remain passive and receptive to ideas and be guided by the Sage.
5 Concentrate upon what you know to be true and right for you.
4 Keep yourself to yourself and be reserved in your actions and words.
3 Be inspired by others but do not trumpet your own achievements.
2 Respond to circumstances as they arise with suppleness and adaptability.
1 Use this time to consolidate what you learn and to develop your inner truth.

屯 3 CHUN – Difficult beginnings *Immaturity, perseverance*

Water

Thunder

This is a time of potential growth, but like any new venture there is often initial adversity. As the seedling perseveres and grows, so will you overcome difficult beginnings if you persevere in holding on to proper principles. A new situation can develop in any direction; by being aware of this possibility you can correct harmful growth before it goes too far. Accept help that is offered and remain steadfast during this chaotic time, allowing it to resolve itself, and your progress will be successful.

Line readings

6 Trust in the guidance of the I Ching and you will win through eventually.
5 Trying to force a resolution will inevitably result in failure.
4 Sincerely ally yourself to others who are also true and sincere, and all will go well.
3 Be cautious and trust your instincts to alert you to hidden hazards.
2 Wait patiently for a solution that is correct in all respects.
1 Progress is difficult but be patient and the way ahead will become apparent.

蒙 4 MÊNG – Youthful folly *Inexperience, guidance, enthusiasm, tuition*

Mountain

Water

Youth is a time of inexperience but it is possible to be old yet inexperienced in a certain area. Youth is also a time of boundless enthusiasm which can lead to folly, but enthusiasm can see you through the setbacks that inexperience can cause. Beginner's luck will eventually run out, however, and to continue to grow it is necessary to seek guidance from an experienced teacher and to learn from your mistakes. The I Ching offers this guidance and its wisdom can help you to learn as you grow.

Line readings

6 Do not dwell on mistakes, but accept the lesson and move on.
5 Be free of arrogance and set ideas and you will benefit accordingly.
4 Experience is learning and the harder the lesson, the greater the benefit.
3 Beware of turning respect and admiration for another into idolatry.
2 Listen to all; it is possible to learn even from those who are inexperienced.
1 Accept criticism and advice that is well founded but maintain your enthusiasm.

5 HSU – Waiting *Correctness, patience, perseverance, nourishment*

Water

Heaven

There is a time for advancement and a time for patient non-action. Now is the time to wait and have faith in the order of things. This image is of clouds gathering before rain can fall. They are the creative potential which will bring nourishment to the land when the time is right. To gather creative energy you must wait with calm patience, maintaining the inner truth that will allow the universe to work. Use this time to observe yourself and to correct any inferior feelings that cause imbalance.

Line readings
6 The situation is coming to a resolution, although perhaps not as you had hoped for.
5 There is always calm in a storm but beware, the situation is not yet resolved.
4 Remain calm and confident that things are as they should be.
3 Do not give in to inner doubts but wait with calmness and discipline.
2 Keep your self-discipline and do not respond to attacks from others.
1 An outside influence is approaching. Prepare yourself by remaining calm and focused.

6 SUNG – Conflict *Opposition, disengagement, communication*

Heaven

Water

Conflict arises from within and the strong connection to heaven is being eroded by the swirling confusion of water. By trying to impose your view instead of accepting what comes, your conflict with the universe attracts external opposition. This clash cannot be overcome by force as confrontation only feeds the ego. Disengage from doubts, fears and impatience, and communicate with others to help resolve conflict. Accept and respect the advice of someone wiser than you in this situation.

Line readings
6 Conflict gives rise to more conflict. In the long run it is better just to let it go.
5 Accept the wisdom of an objective third party and things will work out well.
4 Stay calm and resolved and recognize the pointlessness of conflict.
3 By retaining your integrity and humility you can achieve great things.
2 Calmly pulling back from conflict will bring benefits to all involved.
1 Defuse a situation before it has a chance to get out of hand.

7 SHIH – The army *Unity, harmony, acting in concert, strength, division*

Earth

Water

Dissent in the ranks causes unrest and instability because the leader is overbearing, unjust or weak-willed. An army needs a strong leader who commands respect with compassion, strength and wisdom. You are a divided army because your general is not leading by example. Lack of inner harmony brings disunity to other relationships. Be firm in your purpose and exemplary in your actions and you will be an inspiration to others, gaining their support and achieving a worthy goal.

Line readings
6 Success is yours but you should reflect honestly on how it was gained.
5 Retaliation against disruptive elements should be restrained and understanding.
4 Unless you are working coherently there can be no advancement.
3 Maintain your honesty and integrity and a realistic sense of authority.
2 It is the mutual support between the leader and followers that carries the day.
1 Retain your understanding of justice and correct behaviour.

8 PI – Holding together *Union, bonding, co-operation*

Water

Earth

Harmony – the water soaking into the earth – produces a good harvest. A union needs to be harmonious for the best results, whether the relationship is with yourself or with others. Strengthen bonds by reviewing your actions and demeanour. Are you being truthful? Your position of power doesn't mean that you can do what you like. However, it does require steadiness of principle in the face of challenges and temptations. Maintain your inner truth and sincerity and you will achieve much.

Line readings
6 Proceed cautiously but do not hesitate to enter a beneficial union.
5 Don't sink to coercion or flattery to hold on to someone who wants to go.
4 Be yourself and feel free to express your thoughts and feelings more.
3 Be wary of joining with people who may lead you astray.
2 Do not be swayed by inferior principles just to keep the image of harmony.
1 Lack of truth, in yourself or with others, leads to disunity.

小畜 ## 9 HSIAO CH'U – Taming by the small *Patience, strength*

Wind

Heaven

Others recognize who you are and what you stand for, but not sufficiently to allow trouble-free advancement. Forcing your way is beneath you and will only bring misfortune. The only way to progress is to remain focused and seek to remove obstacles with gentle actions. Look to the long term rather than to immediate satisfaction; by planting seeds now you will reap a rich harvest in future. Cultivate patience, adaptability and detachment, and accept that all you can do is change yourself.

Line readings
6 Success is imminent. Keep to the correct principles to ensure its arrival.
5 If you share your good fortune with others it will be increased.
4 Retreat from confrontations, even if you are misunderstood, and things will work out well.
3 Do not let doubts or over-confidence tempt you to force an issue.
2 Remain firm and devoted to your inner truth and all will come right.
1 Impatience causes despair and hasty actions, which will not benefit you.

履 ## 10 LU – Conduct *Caution, courtesy, simplicity, innocence*

Heaven

Lake

The allusion is to stepping on a tiger's tail: overstepping the mark and causing offence. Be aware of caution and restraint. If you conduct yourself with humility and good humour, it is possible to walk on the most dangerous ground with a degree of safety. By maintaining simplicity of thought and deed, and innocent expression of your inner truth, others will accept you for who you are. Do not be subservient to those above nor domineering to those below and you will meet with success.

Line readings
6 True achievement is measured in the manner of attainment as well as in the rewards gained.
5 Be resolute and determined with yourself but not hard and judgemental with others.
4 Do not be tempted to avert or interfere with a difficult situation; just leave it alone.
3 Don't over-estimate yourself or your abilities, allow things to develop as they will.
2 You know what is correct; doubts and questions will only bring trouble.
1 Step lightly with quiet confidence and without ambition to ensure smooth progress.

泰 ## 11 TAI – Peace *Balance, harmony, new growth, prosperity*

Earth

Heaven

Your inner harmony is reflected in the peace around you. Earth above indicates an open attitude to events, and heaven below suggests a time of burgeoning potential. In such fertile ground it is possible to grow to great heights but you need to maintain your inner balance. Most spiritual growth comes through challenging times: do not relax into complacency just because times are good. To develop new growth potential you need to remain devoted to the correct principles of the I Ching.

Line readings
6 Good fortune fades, to be replaced by a time of learning. Accept what comes calmly.
5 Maintain your inner calmness and patience; things are progressing as they should.
4 Do not boast to others or try to manipulate them as this will lead to your downfall.
3 Keep your equanimity in difficult times because they will change.
2 Be generous and forbearing and do not allow good fortune to cloud your judgement.
1 Others are attracted by your positivity. Welcome them and act together.

否 ## 12 P'I – Standstill *Lack of progress, barriers, stagnation*

Heaven

Earth

P'i is the reverse of Tai (11), indicating that the creative is leaving and the receptive is rising. The run of good fortune has waned and now comes a time of stagnation. This lack of progress does not mean that you cannot develop your inner truth. Be receptive to the lessons and don't struggle against those who hold the upper hand because that will only serve to make them stronger. Retreat into yourself and have faith that things will improve faster if you persevere in the correct manner.

Line readings
6 By acting with a pure heart and honest intent you will meet with good fortune.
5 Adhere to your higher principles to strengthen your inner truth.
4 Acting in a pure and simple manner will bring benefits and support from others.
3 Make no judgements of others but do what you know to be right.
2 Times are hard but the best way to proceed is by enduring.
1 Withdraw from an adverse situation and wait patiently for better times.

13 T'UNG JÊN – Fellowship with others *Co-operation*

Heaven

Fire

A union of equals comes together to work towards a mutual goal, with no reservations or hidden agendas. To function coherently requires openness, honesty and a sense of fairness felt by all. If there are reservations within the group it will not work. These need to be addressed if you are to continue or a state of chaos will prevail. This hexagram also refers to joining with the Sage, being sincerely committed to seeking the wisdom and truth without regard to having it proven to yourself.

Line readings
6 Good fortune will come if you wholeheartedly embrace the wisdom of the Sage.
5 Bonds based on love and respect are unbreakable and reconciliation will come.
4 Misunderstandings lead to trouble. It is better to disengage than to continue fighting.
3 Feelings of mistrust will grow and break the union unless dealt with quickly.
2 Creation of factions within the group will lead to failure.
1 For a union to endure there needs to be openness between the parties involved.

14 TA YU – Possessing plenty *Wealth, abundance, honour*

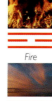

Fire

Heaven

By following true and honest intentions you are entering a period of great abundance, from which you can shine like a fire in the heavens. You have reached this point by retaining your humility and integrity. Carry on in this manner and you will continue to rise and prosper, becoming a guiding light for others. It is important to guard against unworthy thoughts and actions or seeking to use your influence to further your own ends. If you abuse your strength it will be lost to you.

Line readings
6 Continue with modesty and humility and great abundance will come.
5 Do not be effusive or stand-offish but accept people with a quiet dignity.
4 Rise above petty competition and you will continue on your ascent.
3 Do not hoard your wealth, spiritual or material, because that leads to stagnation.
2 Remain free of attachments because possessions can become fetters.
1 Do not be waylaid by feelings of arrogance or superiority as your good fortune continues.

15 CH'IEN – Modesty *Quietly progressing, steadfast, developing*

Earth

Mountain

Strive to remain modest in your dealings. The image of the mountain below the earth is one of curtailing ostentatious behaviour to deepen and develop the inner self. Modesty is about perceiving what is good and right, and being steadfast in acting upon it and following those actions through. If you maintain awareness and follow the correct path, deeper contact with the Sage and with your inner truth is forged, strengthening you and enabling you to face any obstacles with calm confidence.

Line readings
6 A truly modest person knows what is right and has the strength to follow it.
5 You may have to assert yourself but do so without resorting to aggression.
4 Do what needs to be done quietly, efficiently and with respect.
3 Modesty brings success and attention. Do not become complacent or conceited.
2 Others recognize a deep modesty in you and react accordingly.
1 True modesty brings its own rewards. Do not expect recognition for your actions.

16 YU – Enthusiasm *Energy, opportunity, support*

Thunder

Earth

This is a good time to start a new undertaking. Your boundless enthusiasm provides the energy and strength to see it through and your vigour will communicate to others, who will join with you and lend their support. However, the enthusiasm needs to be derived from a strong inner clarity of what is right and what needs to be done. If it springs from an egotistical desire to be seen to be successful, you will become unbalanced and the energy will not be sufficient to carry you through.

Line readings
6 Enthusiasm springing from the desires of the ego will lead to misfortune.
5 Look within to determine if you carry the seeds of doubt.
4 Maintaining a correct enthusiasm for your endeavours will lead to success.
3 You know what is best so you can rely on your own judgement.
2 Retain a sense of propriety and a realistic view of what can be done.
1 An arrogant manner towards others will prove to be your undoing.

隨 17 SUI – Following *Acceptance, following, joy*

Lake

Thunder

A fundamental principle of the I Ching is an acceptance of what is, while maintaining equanimity in response to events. This hexagram relates to following and being followed. The principles of the I Ching arouse the interest of a follower and adherence to the principles of humility, inner truth and acceptance, lead to joy. Other people see the joy in a true follower and their interest is aroused. To show them the way to true joy you must remain steadfast to the principles of the Sage, the I Ching.

Line readings

6 Being receptive to the principles of the Sage brings what is needed at the right time.
5 By being true to yourself you ensure great success because the universe assists you.
4 Do not let flattery go to your head or your clarity will become clouded.
3 It may be time to part from people or ideas that conflict with your inner knowledge.
2 Inferior attitudes will prevent you hearing wisdom from truly wise people and the Sage.
1 Wisdom can come from unexpected sources. Be respectful and listen to all.

蠱 18 KU – Work on corruption *Disruption, decay, spoiled, repairing*

Mountain

Wind

The ideogram represents decay and corruption. The hexagram portrays wind blowing around the base of the mountain, a deep-rooted disorder. However, there is a chance to redeem the situation by correcting improper attitudes and ideas. This will take strength of character and decisive action but first it is necessary to ascertain the root cause, which requires a period of meditation and introspection. Once established, work quickly to repair the damage and guard against its return.

Line readings

6 Following the path of inner truth may isolate you but this will not be permanent.
5 Your efforts at repair have been noticed by others, who may be inspired to aid you.
4 Deal with the corruption now to avoid further disruption.
3 An excessive approach has led to a minor upset but no great harm has been done.
2 Use gentle persistence to address the decay. Excessive vigour will increase disruption.
1 Decay in this case is coming from a pattern learned rather than from an inner voice.

臨 19 LIN – Approach *Advance, waxing power, strength, benevolence*

Earth

Lake

This hexagram refers to what is approaching you and how you approach life. There are good times coming imminently and any undertaking you begin will be successful. This is because you have cultivated the correct internal equanimity and the higher powers approach you to give assistance. Just because times are good you should not relax the inner discipline that has brought about your success. If you do, the progress that has begun will halt and your good fortune will melt away.

Line readings

6 You have reached a point of development where you are able to help others.
5 Don't interfere or have doubts about the abilities of those helping you.
4 An open-minded attitude towards others will ensure success.
3 Keep your attitudes to yourself and others under control to ensure continued progress.
2 The correct approach will help you through the bad times that follow the good times.
1 Fortunate circumstances make your progress seem effortless; maintain discipline.

觀 20 KUAN – Contemplation *Meditation, understanding, example*

Wind

Earth

By contemplating or meditating upon the principles of the I Ching, those attributes become a part of your make-up and you become a guiding light for all to see. The creative power of the universe also works in unseen ways, influencing situations and people without conscious intent. This position of strength has been attained by perseverance in adhering to inner correctness. It allows the universal energy to transmute petty aspects of the self into tolerance, patience and understanding.

Line readings

6 Your contemplation has achieved the desired results in yourself.
5 Contemplation furthers your understanding but only becomes wisdom in practice.
4 Your wisdom can have a positive influence on others but do not force it on them.
3 You have enough self-awareness to recognize when improper responses to life arise.
2 Do not expect to make great leaps forward. Gradual progress is inexorable and lasts.
1 Just because you follow the teachings of the Sage you cannot expect others to do so.

21 SHIH HO – Biting through *Clarity, decisiveness, obstacle, unity*

Fire

Thunder

An obstruction is preventing a mouth from closing properly to allow nourishment. There is an obstacle, which could be an incorrect attitude that needs to be dealt with now. You need clarity to see the problem and decisiveness of action to "bite" through it. This does not mean using aggressive force because an overly robust response will bring misfortune. Return to the principles of correctness laid out in the I Ching. Use your inner strength to withdraw and embrace the Sage.

Line readings
6 Severe misfortune will be the result of persisting stubbornly.
5 Stay impartial and objective in order to respond correctly to others.
4 You begin to see progress in dealing with the problem. Maintain your balance.
3 You are faced with an old problem. The correct way to deal with it is to withdraw.
2 In responding to an obstacle you may have gone too far but there is no great harm done.
1 This is a new obstacle, a first offence. Be lenient in how you deal with it.

22 PI – Grace *Adornment, beauty, simplicity*

Mountain

Fire

Grace is perfect poise, beauty and balance. True grace comes from a firm inner truth, humility and acceptance, whereas false grace relies on external appearances to beautify the self for the appeasement of the ego. Grace is the embodiment of nature and possesses a beauty that is effortless. Similarly, a person who does not try to be alluring but cultivates devotion to the simplicity of the inner truth of the Sage possesses a grace and beauty that shines through the dowdiest of coverings.

Line readings
6 The external trappings of success are false. True power and grace shine from within.
5 Concentrate on simplicity and sincerity and don't be tempted to seek material wealth.
4 Do not try to impress others with an outward show of brilliance.
3 All seems well but don't fall into complacency and arrogance.
2 Cultivate an ability to see through surface adornment to perceive underlying integrity.
1 Let modesty be your guide to inner truth.

23 PO – Splitting apart *Strong, enduring, patient, non-action*

Mountain

Earth

Everything seems to be going horribly wrong, but nothing can be done about it except to weather the storm. To attempt to influence the situation will only prolong it because such a desire is driven by the ego, which seeks to dominate and control. By withdrawing from unfavourable circumstances and engaging in patient non-action the creative power can settle the situation favourably. Be like the mountain, strong and immovable, resting solidly on the earth of your proper principles.

Line readings
6 Do not dwell on what has passed but step forward with optimism into better times.
5 By accepting what comes conditions become more favourable.
4 The storm has reached its peak. Cling to correct principles and endure it.
3 Anchor yourself to the Sage's principles. Don't worry about opposition from others.
2 Resist the urge to interfere and have patience. This situation won't last indefinitely.
1 Acting in response to fear and doubt will end in disaster. Things are as they should be.

24 FU – Return *Change, turning point, improvement*

Earth

Thunder

Just as the winter solstice presages the returning power of the sun, this hexagram, which is related to that time of year, tells of a time of increasing fortune. It is also a reminder to look for the light of inner truth to guide your path. In the same way that the seasons progress in an inexorable cycle, so too do the ebb and flow of fortune and misfortune. Watch and wait as things progress and develop at their own rate, and draw in your strength for the time of growth that is approaching.

Line readings
6 Now is the time for careful self-evaluation and for correcting improper attitudes.
5 If you are moved to excuse your behaviour, you are aware that you are in the wrong.
4 In going your own way you may have to offend others. True friends will understand.
3 Change can be frightening but there is no gain if you keep returning to bad habits.
2 Be careful of allowing your pride to stop you from learning from others.
1 Be aware when you stray from a true and honest path and return before you go too far.

25 WU WANG – Innocence *Purity, present moment, sincerity, intuition*

Heaven

Thunder

Innocence is living purely in the present, as a child does, with no thought of tomorrow or yesterday. The innocent child accepts the guidance of the wiser adult and trusts that all will be well. Develop innocence so that there is no anticipation of events and no holding on to what has passed, good or bad. The pure spirit, the higher self, is directly connected to the rest of creation. If you nurture it, intuition flows and it is possible to follow the guidance of the wiser adult, the Sage, as it leads us through life.

Line readings
6 Do not try to force an issue but step back and let the truth unfold.
5 Remain innocent and detached and a problem will quickly pass on its own.
4 Stay true to yourself and be guided by the teachings of the Sage.
3 Stay calm and strengthen your innocence in the face of a misfortune.
2 Do not dwell on past mistakes or anticipate future goals.
1 Trust your first instincts because intuition flows from the cosmos.

26 TA CH'U – Taming by the great *Keeping still, practice*

Mountain

Heaven

It is a time to put into practice the teachings of the I Ching. To remain calm and detached in the face of hostile provocations is a great test of the strength of your character. Hold firmly to the sense of inner truth – the power of the great – and use the difficulties as opportunities to increase your understanding by purifying your thoughts and actions. These attacks may come from people who are jealous and fearful of your spiritual progress, or from inner aspects of yourself that clamour for attention.

Line readings
6 Creative energy released and guided by your correct behaviour will bring success.
5 Acting out of desire causes great disruption to your equanimity. Stay calm and detached.
4 Curb actions that arise from strong emotions and you will know the time to act.
3 Proceed with determination and caution because there are still problems ahead.
2 By staying calm you conserve your energy for greater advantage when the time is right.
1 Staying patient in a difficult situation will bring a quicker resolution.

27 I – The corners of the mouth *Discipline, meditation*

Mountain

Thunder

The image of the hexagram is a mouth, open and ready to receive nourishment. As healthy food nourishes the body, healthy thoughts and actions nourish the spirit. By feeding on the desires of the ego you promote the growth of inferior spiritual qualities. Meditation is a way to cultivate a tranquil, receptive state that allows wisdom to flow from the universe, nourishing your higher self and influencing others positively as the peace and tranquillity it instils radiates outwards.

Line readings
6 Others turn to you for guidance. Remain humble and sincere in your dealings.
5 Strengthen your discipline and follow the Sage before you try to help others.
4 You will receive help by seeking to nourish yourself in the proper manner.
3 Feeding on desires is never fulfilling because there is always something else to be had.
2 Seeking nourishment from others will weaken you and bring misfortune.
1 You have everything you need, so you should be content with it.

28 TA KUO – Preponderance of the great *Pressure, growth*

Lake

Wind

This hexagram indicates a situation of almost unbearable pressure and it seems likely that you will give way beneath the weight. There is an understandable temptation to escape and seek a refuge, but that only delays the inevitable. To keep running only weakens your resolve. Now is the time to stand firm. You are equal to the task and by relying on your inner truth and integrity you will emerge stronger. This may require a sacrifice on your part to bring a wider benefit to others.

Line readings
6 You are in over your head because of over-confidence. Return to patience and humility.
5 To progress in a renewed relationship the problems undermining it must be resolved.
4 Do not exploit the respect that others have for you or there will be cause for regret.
3 Stop your headlong rush, which is propelling you towards disaster.
2 This is a time of renewal. Things will go well if you stay alert and proceed cautiously.
1 Be cautious as you advance and test each step. Do not fear to pull back from danger.

坎 **29 K'AN – The abysmal** *Depths, despair, danger, alertness*

Water

Water

Flowing water follows the path of least resistance on its journey from the heavens to the sea. The doubling of water indicates depths of despair, dangerous chasms created by giving in to strong emotions that urge you to seek an easy solution. Other depths within yourself, if plumbed, can provide the strength to see you through difficulties. Flow with the current of change instead of struggling against it. Open your heart and be receptive to allow the universe to work out the best solution.

Line readings
6 Your predicament comes from ignoring what you know is right. Listen to your heart.
5 A thing will come to fruition when it is ready. Stop striving and go with the flow.
4 Be sincere in all your thoughts and actions and help will come to you.
3 Any movement is dangerous. Retreat into stillness until a solution presents itself.
2 Slowly and cautiously is the way to find your path through the abyss that faces you.
1 Be alert to danger or bad habits and return to the path of peaceful acceptance.

離 **30 LI – The clinging** *Dependence, passion, brilliance, intensity*

Fire

Fire

Fire gives warmth, illumination and simple beauty burning with a captivating intensity. But fire depends upon wood to give it form, and clings to it with passion. You depend on external things for your survival, but there is another dimension that gives you a passion for life, and that is a spiritual connection to the rest of creation. Clinging to correct principles gives us the strength to live a joyful and fulfilling life, able to face difficulties with equanimity and paradoxically to gain independence.

Line readings
6 The ego still holds sway and needs to be silenced before progress can be made.
5 Be humble and accepting in the face of adversity and good fortune will be yours.
4 Perseverance will bring its rewards.
3 Accepting that things come in their own time allows their healthy development.
2 Do not succumb to despair or over-exuberance. Moderation in all things will bring good fortune.
1 Listening to desires and inferior attitudes leads to misfortune.

咸 **31 HSIEN – Influence** *Harmony, mutual benefit, unifying, courtship*

Lake

Mountain

This hexagram indicates the approach of an influence. The constituent trigrams represent the third son and the third daughter, suggesting courtship. This involves following the correct procedure to bring about a joyful and mutually beneficial union. To be able to receive benefits from external influences you must be open-minded and gentle. To have a beneficial influence on others we need to maintain our inner independence and integrity, acting from a position of quiet inner truth and humility.

Line readings
6 Let your knowledge become deeds and they will have more influence than words alone.
5 You need a strong will to hold firm to your inner truth but beware of being too rigid.
4 By always speaking and acting with integrity you will have a positive influence on others.
3 Desire can cause you to act rashly or to seek to use your influence for selfish gains.
2 Have patience. Correct progress takes time and to act now will lead to misfortune.
1 Maintain a firm discipline in the early stages of an influence and success will be easier.

恆 **32 HÊNG – Duration** *Persistence, progress, endurance, stamina*

Thunder

Wind

This is a time of endurance, which requires persistence and stamina. By calling upon the enduring principles of calmness, humility and sincerity, you will achieve success. You may be going through a change, but the counsel of this hexagram is to hold your equanimity. Do not wish or hope for something to be better or fear that things will get worse, but remain constant and unwavering in your actions as you deal with the situation, doing what needs to be done with calmness, detachment and integrity.

Line readings
6 Stay calm and in the present to allow the creative energy of the universe to work.
5 Allow others to make their own way, learning through their own experiences.
4 What you seek will not be found if you look in the wrong places or in the wrong way.
3 Do not measure yourself against others but remain strong and certain in your path.
2 Your intuition flows through your higher self. Trust in it to guide you.
1 Expecting too much too soon leads to disappointment. Stay focused on the present.

33 TUN – Retreat *Withdrawal, conserving strength, stillness, order, safety*

Heaven

Mountain

There is a natural ebb and flow of energy, which the discerning person recognizes and accepts. Faced with the onset of winter, a tree does not put forth new growth but draws in its strength and waits for spring. When there are superior forces marshalled against you, it is best to retreat into calm stillness and to conserve and organize your strength. Retreat is acceptance of unfavourable odds, performing a strategic withdrawal in order to make preparations for a more favourable time to advance.

Line readings
6 You are correct in retreating and your path will open up before you.
5 You have seen the wisdom of retreating now and must act decisively.
4 A correct retreat will only strengthen you.
3 Don't allow others to interfere with your priority to withdraw.
2 A fair and proper resolution cannot come about if you demand it or interfere to try to change the situation.
1 Withdraw from a negative situation now and take no further action.

34 TA CHUANG – Power of the great *Strength, heaven*

Thunder

Heaven

This is a time of increasing strength, but you must guard against complacency. You reach this position with the help of the Sage. In following the correct principles of patience, humility, gentleness and detachment, you align yourself with the creative forces of the universe and can achieve great things. Remember the other counsels: reticence, timeliness and balance. If, through a misguided belief in your power, you seek to use this influence to benefit your own ends, the resulting misfortune will be great.

Line readings
6 Pressing forward without due consideration can lead to entanglements that will hinder you.
5 It is sometimes necessary to be harsh but do not carry the punishment too far.
4 Remain true to your principles: resistance will crumble and good fortune is assured.
3 Use your strength wisely, not as a battering ram. Advance when there is no resistance.
2 Gentle persistence will lead to further progress so maintain discipline in easy times.
1 Don't be tempted to use your power to force issues to a conclusion.

35 CHIN – Progress *Advancement, dawning, rising*

Fire

Earth

Fire over earth represents sunrise and indicates great progress. The sun climbs effortlessly in the sky because it follows the natural laws of the universe. The growth of your understanding and influence will also be easy if you remember where the light of your brilliance comes from and follow the guidance of the Sage. Clouds can obscure the sun and your judgement can become clouded if you do not work for progress for its own sake rather than in the pursuit of selfish goals.

Line readings
6 Treating others harshly to teach them a lesson is an abuse of your power.
5 Progress is not always obvious but by remaining detached you have made great gains.
4 Using your power for selfish gains or material possessions will lead to misfortune.
3 It is not weak to receive help. Keep to your path truly and accept aid gratefully.
2 Don't compromise your principles for the sake of a union.
1 Progress seems slow in coming but keep your faith and gains will accrue.

36 MING I – Darkening of the light *Oppression, inner light*

Earth

Fire

Earth over fire represents sunset, a time of approaching darkness, when the only light left is inner brightness. When you are engulfed by difficult circumstances, it is necessary to keep that inner light bright to guide you. Giving in to weakness or indulging in feelings of despair dims the brightness within. Now, more than ever, is a time for detachment and perseverance at maintaining an inner truth. Things progress slowly but progress they do, so have faith in the creative power of the universe.

Line readings
6 Hold fast to your true path and firm your resolve, and you will win through.
5 There is no shame in hiding your true self from those who may wish you harm.
4 Realizing you are on the wrong path enables you to leave it. To stay is foolish.
3 Identifying the problem is only half the job. Persevere in dismantling the blockage.
2 Accept aid that is offered and, in turn, be unstinting in your efforts to help others.
1 Detach yourself from a desire for progress and continue with patient perseverance.

I Ching

37 CHIA JÊN – The family *Harmony, loyalty, health, balance, structure*

Wind

Fire

For a family to be successful it needs a firm structure with a strong, honest leader and harmonious relationships. This togetherness stems from mutual love, respect and loyalty, so that there is a willingness to put the welfare of the whole above individual desires. This firm foundation is essential for the health of all human communities and needs to start with the individual. By cultivating the correct principles of acceptance, humility, modesty and gentleness you attract and develop healthy relationships.

Line readings

6 Good fortune will be yours if you keep your actions and thoughts correct.
5 Your influence will be greater if you act out of truth rather than by trying to force issues.
4 Ensure your actions are for the right reasons, not based upon inferior emotions.
3 Be fair but firm when dealing with others. Weakness or aggression will bring misfortune.
2 Do not resort to bullying or aggression to get your own way.
1 Set clear boundaries; if people know their limits they can act more freely within them.

38 K'UEI – Opposition *Misunderstanding, resistance, adversity*

Fire

Lake

Opposition arises through misunderstandings and this is because people, events or situations are judged by their external appearances. If you feel that life is not fair because it is not what you desire, you misunderstand the way the universe works. Resisting the flow of creative energy only increases the power of such inferior attitudes. Everything that comes to you is appropriate for your learning and spiritual growth, but this can only be discerned by looking for the lessons within.

Line readings

6 You feel threatened by others or by life but your paranoia is unfounded.
5 Openness and understanding will allow a firm relationship to grow.
4 Trust in the universe and keep an open heart and you will meet like-minded people.
3 Circumstances seem against you but all is as it should be, so look for the lesson.
2 Understanding can be overlooked unless you receive everyone and everything openly.
1 Accept what comes. Do not chase dreams or people as that will only drive them away.

39 CHIEN – Obstruction *Obstacles, barriers, blockage, stuck*

Water

Mountain

When faced with obstacles, you may indulge in self-pity or seek to overcome them forcibly. These attitudes only make the obstruction seem even more insurmountable. If you give in to these emotions, you block the assistance of the higher self. There is no point in blaming others for the predicament, the answers will come from looking within. It is best to retreat from the problem and examine the self for attitudes that need correcting, and to seek advice from a wise friend or counsellor.

Line readings

6 Others may need your help. Do not forsake them even if the difficulties seem too great.
5 The current situation is hard work but by persevering you will receive help.
4 If you wait correctly, you will gain what is needed to make advance easier.
3 Take time to consider the matter carefully before acting.
2 Don't waste yourself blaming others for an obstruction that is not of your making.
1 Forging ahead will make things worse. Easy advancement will come when the time is right.

40 HSIEH – Deliverance *Relief, release, growth, progression*

Thunder

Water

Thunder and water together suggest a great thunderstorm that purges and refreshes. Look within when faced with obstacles and seek to correct improper attitudes. Because of the work you have done on yourself, you are being released and the way is clear for steady progression. Now is a time to step forward with confidence and balance. Don't brood on what has gone but forgive and forget any past harms that have been done, accepting them as lessons needed to reach this point.

Line readings

6 There is a last vestige of ego preventing complete deliverance. Let it go and be free.
5 Deliverance comes from firm rejection of old habits and inferior influences.
4 Don't cling to old ideas or acquaintances that may halt your progress.
3 Do not succumb to pride and arrogance lest you undo all your good work.
2 Use your wisdom to see through false praise, which will halt your progress.
1 An obstacle has been overcome. Take time to reflect on it and ensure it does not return.

損 41 SUN – Decrease *Discipline, simplicity, limited, drawing in, restriction*

Mountain

Lake

Decrease is not necessarily a bad time, it is simply another state in the constant flux of life. Everyone reaches a point where energies need to be garnered to avoid depleting them further. A period is coming which requires a return to simplicity. It is a time for restricting the demands of the ego to strive for success or the attainment of goals. Power is limited but, by drawing in and exercising firm discipline, it is possible to rely on the inner strength available to get through the lean period.

Line readings
6 Persevering on the path of honesty and sincerity will bring success.
5 Good fortune will come by following what is true and correct in yourself.
4 If you adopt a humble and sincere attitude you will attract others to you.
3 Releasing inferior elements will allow beneficial aid to come.
2 Do not compromise yourself to help others; to do so will be to the detriment of all.
1 If others seek your aid, give it with love and humility but do not over-extend yourself.

益 42 I – Increase *Improvement, gain, progress, assistance*

Wind

Thunder

Like decrease, increase is an inevitable state in the endless cycle of changes. Now is a time when great progress can be made. When you persevere on a path of correctness, the creative power invigorates you. Beware of complacency and remember the source of your good fortune. Be generous and sincere in sharing it with others. This will draw out what is good in them and they will support you. Strengthen your inner resolve and be firm in eliminating inferior elements in your character.

Line readings
6 It is beneficial to give assistance when it is requested of you.
5 Kindness brings its own respect and recognition without being sought.
4 If your guidance as a mediator is sought, be gracious and sincere in the role.
3 Even mistakes turn out well, but learn from them so that they are not repeated.
2 An open acceptance of the workings of fate means that no obstacles can stand before you.
1 By remaining selfless you will bring the success that you seek.

夬 43 KUAI – Breakthrough *Resoluteness, determination, resistance*

Lake

Heaven

A breakthrough comes if you are resolute in dealing with the inferior influences of the ego. By resisting emotional responses, it is possible to defuse them before they become too great. This allows the creative higher powers to flow, unfolding destiny propitiously. Once the breakthrough has occurred, you must remain resolute, and not resort to other inferior expressions such as pride, arrogance or complacency. If these enter, the Sage will withdraw and other obstructions will be experienced.

Line readings
6 The breakthrough has come about and success seems assured. Maintain your discipline to carry it on.
5 Do not judge those who behave incorrectly; they must make their own mistakes.
4 There is a danger that resoluteness will turn to hardness and intolerance.
3 Do not be provoked into action.
2 By remaining cautious and watchful, you will see dangers approaching.
1 Be aware of your own limitations and don't be over-confident.

姤 44 KOU – Coming to meet *Caution, temptation, tolerance*

Heaven

Wind

Be non-judgemental, sincere and humble when meeting the Sage or other people. This gives you the ability to deal with any mishaps calmly and efficiently. There is also a warning here not to meet inferior elements halfway and thus allow them to develop from a weak position to one of growing strength. It is a time for self-examination to test the correctness of ideas, situations and potential allies. If your suspicions are aroused, listen to them because they come from the higher self, which knows what is best.

Line readings
6 Withdraw from the challenges of inferior elements in others who are hostile.
5 Trust in your inner truth and don't use your understanding to berate or impress others.
4 Don't dismiss others out of hand, no matter how offensive they may be.
3 If you feel under attack, retreat into stillness to avoid extending the conflict.
2 Aggressive resistance of inferior emotions will only make them stronger.
1 Negative influences should be nipped in the bud while they are still weak.

45 TS'UI – Gathering together *Peace, prosperity, leadership*

Lake

Earth

When a group acts together towards a well-defined goal, the whole is greater than the sum of the parts. For such a union to prosper, however, requires a strong leader. To be such a leader means gathering within oneself the principles of correctness in order to deal with the outside world calmly. Acting from a stable base, he or she will transmit their strengths to their followers without words or coercion, but if their inner truth is not sincere that will be sensed and the support will fade away.

Line readings

6 If you are sincere in your devotion to the correct principles success will be yours.
5 Remain firm in your goals and don't be afraid to go on alone if necessary.
4 Success is assured if you work selflessly for the general good.
3 Be tolerant of outsiders and do not hold grudges against someone who has strayed.
2 Join with people you feel naturally drawn to and trust in the creative higher powers.
1 Make sure your goals are of the highest order and not just self-serving aims.

46 SHÊNG – Pushing upwards *Direction, ascending, growth*

Earth

Wind

The hexagram suggests a sapling growing stronger and great progress can be made by persisting in what is right. A growing tree draws strength from its roots, which indicates that by maintaining a connection with the Sage, the origin of this success, you will remain strong and firmly rooted. Do not be afraid, simply trust and follow the guidance of the Sage, asking for help from those able and willing to give it. Nothing can stand in your way if you push steadily towards the light.

Line readings

6 How a goal is achieved has as much importance, if not more, than the goal itself.
5 Progress may seem slow but have patience, growth is sure and steady.
4 New opportunities approach and success is assured if you maintain your discipline.
3 How far you go depends on how closely you follow the Sage.
2 By sacrificing petty concerns of the ego you will further your growth greatly.
1 The teaching of the I Ching draws you on and by reaching for it you invoke its aid.

47 K'UN – Oppression *Exhaustion, stretched, adversity, endurance*

Lake

Water

The water is below the lake and therefore the lake is dried up. These are testing times with little or no progress. Be steadfast in the principles laid out in the I Ching. Facing this adverse time with equanimity will allow the lake to refill, plugging the leaks that drain away the precious reserves. A great drain on energy and resources, leading to fatigue, is often caused by harbouring untruths, so this is a time for self-assessment. Look within to see if you are being true to your spirit, your path and the Sage.

Line readings

6 The time of oppression is almost over and it is only negative attitudes that hold you back.
5 The oppression is great but have faith in the workings of fate to see you through.
4 A closed mind is the greatest oppression so dispel fixed ideas about yourself or others.
3 The obstacles are within so look to your attitudes and see what may need correcting.
2 Do not wish for more but be grateful for what you have and draw strength from it.
1 Resist the feelings of despondency and look within for inner reserves of strength.

48 CHING – The well *Spiritual nourishment, counsel, guidance, wisdom*

Water

Wind

Water is a fundamental requirement for survival and must be treated with respect. The image of the well in this hexagram refers to the I Ching as a source of spiritual sustenance that is freely available to any who wish to draw from it. But Ching also serves as a reminder to treat that deep wisdom with respect and not to muddy its waters with frivolous queries or indifference. To gain the full benefits, you need to draw from it with sincerity and to accept its guidance wholeheartedly.

Line readings

6 Give of yourself to others and your fortune will be multiplied.
5 Knowledge becomes wisdom only when it is used. Apply your wisdom for the benefit of all.
4 Keep to the principles of the Sage to maintain the quality of your inner truth.
3 You are avoiding what is right for you. Unused talents are wasted.
2 Focus your energy and intent on something worthwhile instead of misusing it.
1 If you neglect yourself, you must not be surprised if others also neglect you.

革 **49 KO – Revolution** *Change, advance, devotion*

Lake

Fire

The ideogram represents an animal's pelt undergoing its seasonal change. Ko signifies that changes are afoot or that attitudes need to be revolutionized to effect progress. Whichever is the case, now is the time to consider yourself deeply, to analyse your motives and instil the necessary change of heart that will set things in motion. Success is assured if you act from a position of selflessness, because this will bring the support needed and give an awareness of the right time to act.

Line readings
6 The major change is done. Now is a time for fine-tuning in order to carry the change on.
5 Actions based on proper principles make you stand out and others will follow.
4 For change to be long-lasting your motives need to be pure.
3 Don't act too hastily or be too hesitant, but remain balanced and follow your intuition.
2 Prepare yourself carefully before making any radical changes.
1 Develop your inner strength carefully before making your move.

鼎 **50 TING – The cauldron** *Growth, sacrifice, nourishment*

Fire

Wind

Ting derives its name from the image created by the hexagram. The bottom line is the legs of the cauldron, the next three the belly, the fifth the handles, and the top line the lid. The cauldron was the heart of a household: if it was full of food there was sufficient for everyone. This hexagram is related to Ching (48) because it is about providing nourishment, but whereas the Well is about individual spiritual growth, Ting is more about developing what is good within you for the benefit of society at large.

Line readings
6 Lead others by your own example in being open, honest and gentle.
5 Remain modest and sincere and you will receive help in difficult times.
4 Stay alert to potential dangers and don't take on more than you can manage.
3 Don't look for recognition but be patient; just reward comes in its own time.
2 Others may be envious of your success but that cannot harm you.
1 By acting with honesty and purity of intent, success is assured.

震 **51 CHÊN – The arousing** *Shock, movement, stimulation, excitement*

Thunder

Thunder

Thunder piled on thunder represents the incredible power of nature. Is it terrifying? Does that initial jolt give way to excitement or are you unperturbed by momentous events? If you are shocked it indicates that areas or attitudes need looking at. The bigger the shock, the bigger the imbalance. The truly powerful person is unmoved by such occurrences, being in complete harmony with the universal laws. Now is a time to look within and determine where self-correction needs to be made.

Line readings
6 The shock marks the end of the old. Contemplate ways of making a fresh beginning.
5 Shock after shock threatens to unbalance you. Retain your equanimity, all will be well.
4 All movement is blocked; it is a time for stillness and self-evaluation.
3 Use the shock to open your mind and look for possible avenues of action.
2 Let go of possessions and fear. What is really important will be returned.
1 The shock has come as a lesson. Do not be afraid but accept it gratefully.

艮 **52 KÊN – Keeping still** *Stillness, observing, quietness, clarity, readiness*

Mountain

Mountain

Mountain after mountain stretching away into the distance is the very image of stillness. Stillness means not allowing the mind to be ruled by strong emotions because it is not possible to be still with a clamouring mind. What is needed is a calm detachment, observing the emotions but not acting on them, gaining clarity that confers a state of alert readiness. Being alert allows you to see what needs to be done and readiness empowers you to do it, acting when action is needed.

Line readings
6 You are at the peak of the mountain, allowing perfect stillness and clarity.
5 Excessive talking is a sign of a restless mind. Calm your thoughts and speech.
4 If you keep calm and still inside, external influences will have no effect.
3 Don't allow your stillness to be transformed into inflexibility.
2 Don't be pulled along by someone else if it doesn't feel right for you.
1 It is easier to keep still before you move. Be cautious and don't act impulsively.

53 CHIEN – Development *Gradual progress, patience, steady growth*

Wind

Mountain

Wood over mountain represents a tree on a mountainside. In such an exposed environment it needs to have firm roots and to grow gradually, but once it is established it will live long, have an unparalleled view and be visible from a long way off. It is the same for us: to enjoy the benefits of a fine position it is necessary to grow gradually, progressing step by step and learning all the lessons that life brings. The goal may seem a long way off but with patience and diligence it will be arrived at.

Line readings
6 Your progress is visible from afar, serving as an inspiration to others.
5 Your progress may isolate you but it also brings freedom as you continue.
4 Where you are is only temporary but take time to relax before you go on.
3 Rash actions will bring regret. Allow things to develop gradually.
2 Your advance is steady and you can feel secure in sharing your self-development.
1 At the beginning of a journey there is often anxiety. Keep your goal in mind to progress.

54 KUEI MEI – Marrying maiden *Impulsiveness, discipline*

Thunder

Lake

The image called up by this hexagram is that of thunder creating waves on a lake, indicating how desires can lead to the disturbance of equanimity and to impulsive actions. To act on desires is not to follow the principles of the I Ching. There will always be desires and problems in relationships, but Kuei counsels that by following proper conduct they will be minimized. Proper conduct means maintaining detachment, accepting and being wary of compromising principles by following desires.

Line readings
6 You need to be sincere in word and action in your relationships.
5 Be prepared to stand back and let others come to the fore.
4 Be patient and persevere towards your goal.
3 Don't expect too much progress too soon. There is no disgrace in starting out from a lowly position.
2 You may be let down by someone but keep your faith in those you love.
1 With the proper attitude progress is possible, whatever your position.

55 FÊNG – Abundance *Fullness, power, wise actions, plenty*

Thunder

Fire

Thunder and fire represent movement and clarity. They also indicate developing an inner awareness to see your position and to move when the time is right, to take full advantage of these cycles of waxing and waning power. While a thunderstorm fills the sky it is full of power and its influence is felt universally but, like all things, it will pass. Do not look to such a time but live for the present moment, making the most of this period of abundance and influence to achieve great gains.

Line readings
6 Arrogance and conceit will only bring you alienation and misfortune.
5 You can achieve great things with the help of others. Listen to them with respect.
4 Don't get lost in confusion but be guided by your inner clarity.
3 Hold to your inner truth and nothing can stand in your way.
2 Your influence will shine through. There is no need to pretend to greatness.
1 Your inner clarity will know the time to advance and your energy will see you through.

56 LU – The wanderer *Moving, restless, temporary, transient*

Fire

Mountain

The idea of transience comes from the component trigrams which represent a bush fire on a mountain, always seeking more fuel. This can relate to physical travel but it also refers to progressing through life: the best way to proceed on that journey is as if passing through a strange land. When travelling in unfamiliar territory it is wise to be cautious, reserved and respectful, to follow your instincts about places and situations, to carry only what is necessary, with no attachments.

Line readings
6 Be careful of taking your good fortune for granted or it may be lost.
5 Your talents will be recognized more fully if you behave correctly.
4 You are settled for now but you know in your heart that you are not satisfied.
3 Don't involve yourself in something that is really no concern of yours.
2 With the right attitude you will always find a resting place and friends.
1 Remain free of attachments and trivialities and your journey will be much easier.

57 SUN – The gentle *Gentle, penetrating, wind, persistence*

Wind

Wind

To effect any long-lasting change it is necessary to be like a constant gentle wind. When faced with problems it is tempting to take vigorous action, but violent storms wreak havoc and only stir up the local environment. This hexagram advises gentle penetration to dispel any blockages that may stand in your way. To be consistent requires a well-defined goal to focus on, one that can be aimed at with persistent effort. In this way changes will have far-reaching effects and be of a long-term nature.

Line readings
6 To search too hard for inferior elements will cause disruption.
5 Things may have started badly but, if you are duly cautious, they will turn out well.
4 By adhering to your principles and your integrity you will reap great rewards.
3 Dwelling on negative influences gives them more strength. Correct them and move on.
2 Search inside yourself to discover any negative influences.
1 Gentleness does not mean softness. Be sure in your goal and firm in your intent.

58 TUI – The joyous *Inner strength, fulfilment, harmony, joy*

Lake

Lake

You are surrounded by imperatives – to make life better you must have this or must do that – but material gains do not bring lasting joy because there will always be something else to desire. To be fulfilled and live in harmony you need to devote yourself to humility, detachment, modesty and acceptance. By doing this you achieve an independence based on an inner strength which means that, whatever the situation you find yourself in, it can be faced with calm equanimity. That is true joy.

Line readings
6 Following pleasure for its own sake will escalate out of control.
5 You are surrounded by inferior attitudes in yourself and others: do not give in to them.
4 Pursuit of inferior aims brings misfortune. Turn to what is higher for lasting joy.
3 Don't be tempted by material gains, they will soon fade away.
2 If you remain sincere in seeking joy, good fortune will be yours.
1 Release your attachments and experience the joy of freedom.

59 HUAN – Dispersion *Division, dissolution, rigidity, stubbornness*

Wind

Water

Stubborn attitudes lead to harshness and rigidity, blocking the acceptance of people and situations in a free and open manner. This in turn leads to divisions and a lack of unity both within the self and with others. To try and break these fixed ideas forcefully will do no good because they are strong and deep-rooted. The best way to deal with them is to be like the warm spring wind which blows persistently over the winter ice, dissolving it gently and allowing the river to flow freely.

Line readings
6 Don't focus on negative influences or a dangerous situation will develop.
5 A fresh idea can unite people and dispel negativity and misunderstandings.
4 It may be necessary to sacrifice a short-term goal for a long-term benefit.
3 The best way to deal with your problems is to help someone else.
2 Do not judge others harshly. Understanding them will help you understand yourself.
1 Resolve misunderstandings quickly before alienation sets in.

60 CHIEH – Limitation *Restraint, moderation, guidelines, boundaries*

Water

Lake

Limitation is not the same as restriction, rather it means being prudent with resources. In order to be able to use what is available to its fullest potential, you need guidelines. If you know your boundaries you will have a greater freedom of expression within them, because you will know how far you can go with your expenditure. On a physical level you cannot live beyond your means, and similarly on a spiritual level it is wise to restrain desires and fears that are the cause of troubled thinking.

Line readings
6 Severe limitations become restrictive and lead to resentment.
5 Don't enforce limitations on others that you don't follow yourself.
4 Accept natural limitations. Move when you can, stay still when you can't.
3 Be careful of over-extending yourself. You must recognize that you are responsible for knowing your own limits.
2 Do not hesitate, the way is clear.
1 Know your limitations. To press forward now will bring misfortune.

61 CHUNG FU – Inner truth *Prejudice, understanding, acceptance*

Wind

Lake

Prejudices colour the way you relate to life. You cannot reach understanding if you indulge in pride, anger or self-pity. Chung Fu refers to the universal truth, the invisible force that manifests visible effects in life, and the inner truth which also has an invisible influence, good or bad. The I Ching counsels you to leave emotional responses behind and to try to understand the truth of a situation. By doing so your inner truth is emulating the universal inner truth and has a positive influence.

Line readings
6 Trying to persuade others of the right course will do no good. Lead by example and let them make their own way.
5 Inner truth will unite you with others.
4 Do not forget the source of your power when things are going well.
3 To maintain your independence and balance, do not rely on others.
2 Your inner truth, strong or weak, will be felt by others and they will react accordingly.
1 Do not be distracted by others from your inner truth.

62 HSIAO KUO – Preponderance of the small *Non-action*

Thunder

Mountain

This hexagram refers to the dominating presence of inferior attitudes (the small) which makes correct advance impossible. When faced with difficult circumstances it is tempting to be assertive and seek solutions, but this will only make things worse. The best course is patient non-action, relying on the principles of humility, modesty and acceptance to help you. Difficult times always reappear and should be seen for what they are: a test of commitment to the higher principles laid out in the I Ching.

Line readings
6 Pressing forward with something beyond you will bring disaster.
5 Seek help with your problem from someone who is wise and sincere.
4 Be patient and trust that the higher powers are working things out.
3 Show proper caution and don't expose yourself to risks.
2 You have made a small advance; be content with it for now.
1 To act now will bring misfortune. Bide your time and wait for a better opportunity.

63 CHI CHI – After completion *Order, balance, awareness*

Water

Fire

All the lines in this hexagram are perfectly balanced; out of chaos comes order, but this can change in an instant. Although this hexagram indicates hard work culminating in a time of order, there is a warning not to relax the discipline that has got you this far. Maintain an awareness of inferior elements that may arise and tumble the order into chaos again. If these are not recognized and dealt with before they manifest themselves, they will quickly swamp you and undo all your good work.

Line readings
6 Don't look back over past achievements but keep your eye to the future and move on.
5 Simplicity, both in thought and action, is the best way forward.
4 Minor setbacks are warnings of indiscipline, so pay heed to them.
3 To revert to inferior attitudes now will undo all your good work.
2 Remain modest and humble and what you seek will come to you.
1 Keep your discipline and awareness and progress is assured.

64 WEI CHI – Before completion *Caution, potential, clarity*

Fire

Water

This hexagram is the reverse of Chi Chi (63). Here, water is below, moving down, and fire is above, moving up, so the two energies cannot meet and combine. However, they just need to be repositioned so that fire (which represents clarity) can serve as a base for water (which represents action). During regenerative times such as these there is intense pressure to succeed but, to get anywhere worthwhile, you need to proceed cautiously and with firm dedication to higher principles.

Line readings
6 You have gained much but maintain your clarity and don't let things go to your head.
5 Maintain your integrity and perseverance and you will meet with success.
4 The endeavour has begun but there is much to do. You need dedication to reap rewards.
3 It is safe to act but seek help if you don't feel strong enough to do it alone.
2 Do not wait idly for change but prepare yourself for the time to act.
1 You cannot move forward safely without clarity. Impulsive actions bring disaster.

runes

Part of the purpose of life is to learn lessons and gain knowledge and wisdom. Since the dawn of time, humankind has found signs and symbols fascinating and powerful. The power of the runes comes in what they have to teach us. The runes present lessons to us and, if used wisely, can facilitate the learning of those lessons quickly and efficiently.

The runes do not provide the answers to all of life's problems. Neither do they imbue their user with magical powers. They do, however, present signposts for the journey through life. The runes represent certain images, and by working with these, their guidance and teaching becomes accessible to all. The lore of rune-casting was once the domain of a chosen few, when only a minority sought spiritual enlightenment. Today, many people seek answers to questions, and these "seekers of wisdom" should have access to clear instruction regarding this ancient oracle.

This section gives guidance on making and using your own rune set. The imagery and meaning of each rune is featured in an easy reference guide and there are ideas for using and working with runes that go beyond simple divination.

The way of the runes is subtle but powerful and can have a profound effect on many levels. They are used not only for divination, but for protection, healing, empowerment and learning. The mystery of the runes is not a mystery at all, it is simply a path towards greater learning that anyone can tread.

using the runes

To learn from the runes, you need to "tune in" to their vibrations. Each rune has a corresponding tree, colour, herb and crystal which are keys to unlock its lessons. Working with these, you can set up a vibrational field that allows the subconscious mind to learn the vibration and teach its lesson to the conscious mind. Instead of using the conscious mind to try to find the lesson of each rune, you can allow the lesson to find you.

The History of the Runes

The runes were a sacred writing system used throughout the Germanic tribes of northern Europe, especially in Britain, Scandinavia and Iceland. Their origin is uncertain, but runic inscriptions have been found dating from AD 3. The script appears on memorial stones, weapons and tools and its angular style points to the fact that the runes were intended for carving, not writing.

The word "rune" comes from *runa*, meaning "a whisper" or "a secret", which implies a magical use. Throughout northern Europe, shamans existed who evolved a complex and deep spiritual tradition of which the runes were an intrinsic part, and runemasters were held in high esteem. They knew how to practise divination with the runes, and how to use them in magical and healing work.

Learn the lessons of balance and harmony from nature.

Learning from the Runes

Everything in the universe is vibrating; nothing is still. Anything that is balanced and "healthy" has a harmonious vibration. Anything that is unbalanced and "unhealthy" has a discordant vibration. All natural things, such as plants, animals and crystals, have harmonious vibrations. Ultimately human beings are seeking balance and harmony. The runes present symbols whose vibrations help us to become more balanced. They are like a series of lost chords that we need to find. The vibrations of the natural objects associated with them can help us to understand their lessons. They each hold some of the notes of the lost chords.

The ancient Celts and Vikings believed that everything in nature has a "spirit", an energy that can be communicated with and learnt from. This included trees, herbs, crystals, stones and even runes. Through meditation, they were able to "tune in" to their vibrations and learn from them. By meditating with gifts from nature, you will experience their vibrations. The first step is simply to touch, feel, hold, smell and meditate with them. The images and sensations that they offer will become easier to understand as you work with the runes.

Finding your Personal Rune

Hold the bag containing all your runes and empty your mind of all mundane thoughts. Ask the runes to show you your personal power rune which will be your guide. Pick out a single rune from the bag, hold it in your hand and meditate for a while, noting any images and thoughts that enter your mind.

You may wish to wear the corresponding colour and meditate beside the tree while holding the herb and crystal. If you have no access to these, picture them in your mind before you begin to meditate. Ask to be shown some of the lessons that your power rune has to teach you. These will often appear as images that enter your mind and should be noted down. Consider what they may mean, but do not worry if you cannot interpret them all as some of the lessons may only reveal themselves with time and patience. You cannot force understanding.

When you have worked with your power rune for a while, you may wish to research the corresponding tree, colour, herb and crystal – each has healing properties that may give you clues to the areas of your life that need healing and the lessons you need to learn. For example, the oak teaches strength but warns against inflexibility, as it is easily felled in a storm. The willow, on the other hand, teaches this flexibility as it bends in the wind. Even if a piece of it is broken off, that piece will root and grow into a new tree; so it also teaches the power of regeneration.

Meditating with angelica flowers will help you to unlock the meaning of the corresponding power rune, Elhaz.

CONSULTING THE RUNES

Whenever you have a problem for which you can find no solution, a question for which you can find no answer or a decision you cannot make, you can consult the runes. They will not tell you precisely what to do or how to act. But what they will do is comment on a situation, giving you a new perspective from which to view things. This in turn will give you greater objectivity, which will then help you in your decision-making. The wisdom of the runes is more subtle than a simple "yes" or "no" answer. If this is what you want, you will have to flip a coin!

How Divination Works

If you have a problem or an issue for which you need guidance, you can focus your thoughts on that problem while holding your rune bag. This will send a vibration into the runes. The rune or runes that can provide guidance about the issue will resonate, and you will unconsciously be attracted to pick out these runes. The more focused your thinking is, the clearer the answer will be. When focusing on the problem, ask the runes to comment on the issue rather than asking them a "yes" or "no" question.

If, for instance, you are undecided about whether to move into a new house, rather than simply asking the runes, "Should I move into a new house?", you should say, "I would like the runes to comment on the issue of whether or not I should move into a new house." Likewise, if you are asking about a possible partner in love, you should ask the runes to comment on your relationship rather than just asking, "Is this the right person for me?"

Drawing the Runes

Once you have focused on the question you want to ask, you can draw runes in one of two ways. You can pick individual runes out of the bag and lay them on your casting cloth in front of you. Alternatively, you can place all the runes in front of you, face down upon the casting cloth, and pass your hand over them, picking the rune that your hand feels most attracted to. This attraction may manifest itself as a warm, tingling sensation in your hand when it passes over the right rune for you. Once you have chosen a rune, turn it over from left to right and place it in front of you on your casting cloth.

When drawing a rune, it is important that you have a clear intent about the way in which you want the rune to comment. If you wish it to give you a general perspective upon an issue, you need to draw only a single rune. However, you may wish the runes to comment on a number of points relating to a single issue: for example, what has led up to the issue occurring in your life (the past), how you should approach it now (the present) and what the possible outcome could be (the future). In this case, you need to draw three runes, holding one of these aspects clearly in your mind before you draw each rune. In this way you can achieve quite specific guidance which will be of great help to you in coming to a decision about the problem that is concerning you, and more generally on your journey through life.

Interpreting the Runes

The power of interpretation is available to everyone and it improves with practice. There are specific ways to improve your readings and interpretations which will come with patience and a little discipline. Each time you perform a reading with the runes, make a note of the issue on which you are asking the runes to comment, which runes you draw, and what you think they mean. About a month later, go back and look again at the comments you wrote, noting down any new insights that you have gained between the time of the readings and the present. This will help you to evaluate which parts of your original interpretation were accurate, and which were not. In this way, you will be able to improve your skills and understand more clearly what the runes have to say to you, the way that they say it and how you can learn from them.

Drawing a Rune from the Rune Bag

1 Lay out your casting cloth on a table. Concentrate on what you want to ask before you begin to draw the runes. Then pick individual runes out of the bag.

2 Once you have picked a rune out of the bag, turn it over from left to right so that it is face up, and put it down on your casting cloth in front of you.

Picking a Rune from the Casting Cloth

1 Take all the runes out of the bag and place them face down upon the casting cloth. Pass your hand slowly over them to find which runes you are attracted to.

2 When your hand passes over the right rune, it may become warm and tingling. Turn the rune over from left to right and place it in front of you on the casting cloth.

making and caring for your runes

If you want to get to know the runes, it is vital that you create your own rune set, rather than buying one ready-made. This takes time and energy, but it gives you a much more intimate relationship with the runes. The two materials from which runes are commonly made are wood and stone, although other materials, such as crystals, glass beads or clay, can also be used.

Using Wood
The three favoured types of wood for rune-making are ash (the World Tree), yew (the rune Eoh) and birch (the rune Beorc), as they have direct connections to the runes. However, wood from the following trees can also be used for fashioning magical tools and they are listed here with their principal symbology:

Rowan: a protective tree
Willow: a tree very strongly connected with the moon
Oak: symbolic of strength
Hazel: much favoured by diviners
Blackthorn: masculine symbol of spiritual authority
Apple: linked to love
Hawthorn: blackthorn's protective sister tree

Collect 24 stones and paint them with runic inscriptions. Varnish them for protection.

Using Stones
Wherever you go in the world, there are always stones to be found. Some of the best stones for rune-making can be found on beaches and in stream beds, where they have been worn smooth by the water. The Nordic and Celtic people believed that every stone has a spirit within it that needs to be honoured if it is to work well for you, so it is important to leave a small offering at any place where you take something from creation. The traditional offering is sea salt, as it is said to be formed by the fusion of four primal elements – earth, air, fire and water. Alternative offerings include tobacco (which is sacred to the Native Americans), corn (which is sacred throughout the Old World) and coloured ribbon.

Making Runes from Wood
You will need to cut a branch from a living tree to make your rune set. This may be a tree that has special significance to you, perhaps growing in a wood or garden that holds particular memories.

Before cutting any wood from the tree, ask its permission for your act, and leave a small offering in exchange. Select a branch that is about 2–5cm/¾–2in thick. You will need a fairly straight, even length of about 30cm/12in.

1 Ask permission from the tree by placing your hands on its trunk and saying a short prayer.

2 Sprinkle an offering of sea salt at the base of the tree to honour it before cutting off a small branch.

3 Using a handsaw, carefully cut the branch into slices for the 24 runes, about 5mm–1cm/¼–½in thick.

4 Using a poker, a pyrography tool or a soldering iron, carefully burn one runic inscription into each rune.

5 When you have rubbed in a little natural beeswax to protect the wood, your runes are ready to be cleansed.

Cleansing your Runes

When you have finished making your set of runes, it is important to cleanse them spiritually. This can be done in a variety of ways: they can be laid out in the light of a full moon for a night, or you can waft smoking herbs over them (this process is called "smudging"). However, the simplest method of cleansing them is to use naturally flowing water from a well, spring or stream. Do not use tap water as it is full of additional chemicals that are bad for everything, including humans!

As you work with your runes, especially if you do a lot of readings for others, you will need to cleanse them regularly. You may also want to perform an annual re-empowering ceremony. After a while, as you get to know your runes better, they will let you know when they need cleansing: they will start to feel uncomfortable to hold. If this happens, simply re-cleanse them. If your runes have been locked away for any period of time, you will need to re-energize them with the energies of the sun and moon by laying them outside for 24 hours.

Care of your Runes

Runes can be powerful and helpful allies provided that you treat them with the care and respect they deserve. Remember that when you have cleansed and empowered your runes, they will be imbued with your own unique energy and they should never be lent to anyone else for them to use. This does not mean that other people should never touch your runes at all; on the contrary, it is sometimes essential for someone else to touch them, especially if you are giving them a reading and you need them to focus on the runes. But no one else should work with your runes on their own behalf.

To store your runes you will need a bag, which you can make from a piece of natural, unbleached fabric. You can select runes by drawing them one at a time out of the bag. You will also need a piece of natural-coloured fabric to make a casting cloth on which to lay the runes whenever you use them.

Before cleansing your runes, make an offering, then place the runes in a bag and dip them in a stream, for a short while or overnight – let your intuition guide you.

Empowering your Runes

Once you have cleansed your runes, you need to empower them. This can be done in a variety of ways. Some runemasters lay their runes out in the midday summer sun, while others bury them in the earth for nine days. Here, the power of the four elements has been used to empower the runes.

1 Place the runes on a casting cloth and sprinkle them with sea salt to empower the runes with earth.

2 Pass each rune through incense smoke while asking the element of air to empower the runes.

3 Then pass each rune individually through a candle flame to empower the runes with fire.

4 For the final stage, sprinkle a few drops of spring water over the runes to empower them with water.

The Runic Alphabet

The most widely used runic alphabet is the Early Germanic or Elder Futhark, which is used in this book. The word "futhark" refers to the first six runic letters, whose English equivalents are f, u, th, a, r and k. Each runestone depicts one letter from the runic alphabet. The letters of the Elder Futhark are divided into three groups of eight letters, called aetts, as follows:

F U Th A R K G W
H N I J Y P Z S
T B E M L Ng D O

Here is the English alphabet with its equivalent runes (there are no equivalent runes for the letters c, q and v):

A B C D E F G H I J K L M N O P Q R S T U V W X Y Z

interpreting the runes

To become adept at interpreting the runes it is important to train your intuition, the connection to your higher self. This part of you knows your purpose in life and how it can best be achieved. It also knows the purpose of everyone you meet and how best you can guide those people who seek your help. Training the intuition allows you access to that knowledge and the runes can act as catalysts in this process.

Training the Intuition with Meditation
Meditation is a most efficient way of training the intuition because to hear the guiding voice of your higher self, you must have a mind that is in a receptive state to receive those messages. Whenever you pick out a rune to interpret, it is important to meditate with that rune to access your intuition. The following exercise shows you how to do this.

Settle yourself in a place where you feel relaxed; this may be outside if the weather is good, in a place where you feel comfortable and close to nature. If you are planning to consult the runes indoors, sit in a dimly lit room. Make sure that you will not be disturbed by telephones or people. You may wish to light a candle to help you to focus your mind.

Sit down in a comfortable position, hold your rune bag in your hands and close your eyes. Take a few deep breaths to centre yourself and imagine every muscle in your body relaxing. Now you need to empty your mind of all thoughts and to quieten its chatter. Continue to breath steadily and try to focus on your breathing, or picture yourself beside a beautiful lake on a calm, still day. Every time a thought pops into your mind, calmly allow it to leave and refocus upon your breathing or upon the image of the tranquil lake.

Meditating on a Rune
When you feel ready, without opening your eyes, pick a single rune out of the rune bag and hold it in your hand. Keeping your eyes closed, try to tune into its vibration while asking the rune to speak to you. Allow your mind to become open so that different images and thoughts are free to enter it. Remain like this for as long as it feels comfortable. When you feel ready, thank the rune for speaking to you and then open your eyes and look at the rune. Make a note of all the images and messages that came into your mind during your meditation.

Now look up the meaning of the rune and see how this relates to what you felt during your meditation. Note the differences and similarities between the images that you felt during your meditation and the images and lessons given in the book. Now meditate again, asking the rune to show you how all these different images fit together, then note down all your thoughts and impressions.

As you become more experienced at working with the runes, you will be able to review exercises such as the one above and any points that seemed unclear will become clearer as you gain more understanding. The trick is to be patient. The runes reveal different aspects of themselves only when they know you are ready to learn them.

Interpretation of Reversed Runes
Some of the runes reveal a different sign when you view them upside down. These are called reverse runes. If, when you first turn over a rune, you find that you are looking at it upside down, it has a separate meaning to when it is the correct way up. Many people used to regard reversed meanings as negative. For instance, the first rune – Feoh – has an image of wealth and richness, so it was common to regard Feoh reversed as having an image of poverty. This is incorrect.

Each rune has its own lessons to teach. An upright rune has an image that teaches us something. If the rune is reversed, it means that the lessons of the upright rune are what we are lacking and therefore what we need to strive for. Therefore, the image of Feoh reversed does not mean "poverty", but "discovering richness". The difference is subtle but very important. The reversed meanings do not show us problems, but solutions to problems. One should always look at every rune in terms of what it has to teach, rather than looking at the negative aspects of the rune.

Drawing a single rune is a simple way to seek guidance.

divination with the runes

Draw a single rune to act as a guiding rune for the day or before beginning a project, or to gain insight into a problem. It gives an overview of an issue, and is often all the guidance you need. The three-rune spread is particularly useful in giving an overall picture, placing an issue in its context by showing the events that have led up to it, the issue itself and, finally, the most likely future outcome.

THE SINGLE RUNE

Holding your rune bag, focus on the issue upon which you wish the runes to comment. You may say one of the following:
1 "I wish the runes to comment upon the day ahead."
2 "I wish the runes to comment upon (name a future endeavour)."
3 "I wish the runes to comment upon (name an issue or problem)."
Then pick a single rune from the bag or the casting cloth. Meditate while holding that rune, then look up its meaning.

Sample Reading

Tony had just been made redundant from a job that he did not like. Although he was in some ways relieved to be free from it, he was also fearful for his future and was concerned about finding new employment. He asked the runes to comment about this, and drew Rad.

Meaning: The rune Rad means the wheel of life, and signifies that life goes in cycles which will present challenges. Tony learned that he had just come to the end of a cycle in his life. He needed to live in the present and learn its lessons while trusting that the future would provide him only with valuable opportunities to learn more.

After several failed interviews for jobs in the same field as his last one (which anyway he had not enjoyed), he realized that the lesson he should be drawing from his experience was that he needed a different type of job. He decided to look for a job in the open countryside. Here he was much more successful and now thoroughly enjoys his work.

The rune Rad means the wheel of life.

THE THREE-RUNE SPREAD

The three-rune spread is like a signpost at a crossroads. Once you have an issue clearly fixed in your mind, draw your first rune. While focusing on it, think of the events that have led up to the issue or how you have attracted it into your life. Now draw your second rune, and while focusing on it consider the present moment regarding the issue. Finally, draw your third rune, focusing on your wish to be shown where the issue is taking you. Focus on what each rune represents when drawing it. The stronger your focus and intent, the clearer your answers will be.

Sample Reading

Anne had been suffering from ill-health for over six months. She had consulted both medical doctors and alternative health practitioners but to no avail. She did not understand why her illness kept returning, whatever she did to fight it. She drew the following three runes: Geofu, Tyr and Eoh.

Meaning: The rune Geofu means a gift. It showed Anne that her illness was a gift which she was trying to reject instead of accepting. The gift was the lessons the illness had to teach her. Tyr, the warrior god, showed Anne that if she remained true to herself and her beliefs, she would gain victory over her illness. Eoh, the yew tree, stands for transformation, and showed Anne that major change was coming and that by embracing the future while letting go of the past, she would enter a new phase of her life. Anne realized that the cure to her illness lay within her. She dealt with several unresolved issues from the past and was quickly restored to health.

The three-rune spread of Geofu, Tyr and Eoh.

the four-element spread

The runes can be used in many different spreads or patterns to give deep insights to help you on your spiritual path. The spreads are designed to help you understand and learn from the lessons that life is giving you. In the four-element spread, each rune is placed at one of the cardinal points, each of which is associated with one of the four universal elements, Earth, Water, Fire and Air.

The Four Elements

The Nordic tradition views the four elements as the building blocks of the universe, and a different direction and quality are assigned to each element. The north is the place of earth, the west of water, the south of fire, and the east of air. By compiling a spread where the runes are positioned at each point of the compass, each one is imbued with the qualities of its corresponding element.

Sea salt represents Earth, which is grounding and is symbolic of all physical lessons in our lives.

Stream represents Water, which is symbolic of emotional balance and going with the flow through life.

Candle flame represents Fire, which is symbolic of how we express ourselves in our lives and on our spiritual path.

Smoke represents Air, which is symbolic of turning knowledge into wisdom to benefit our future lives.

1 Earth: Situated in the north of the spread, this has a downward, grounding pull and represents all your physical lessons.
2 Water: Positioned to the west, this is an upward and buoyant sign and represents all your emotional lessons.
3 Fire: At the south of the spread, fire represents your spiritual lessons and is closely linked to your unfolding destiny.
4 Air: Positioned to the east, air can draw in knowledge and therefore represents the place where you should go to seek wisdom for the future.

Sample Reading

Jenny had just lost her mother. Although it did not come as a shock, she was still having problems dealing with it. She asked the runes for help and guidance and drew the following: Hagall, Daeg, Is and Feoh reversed.

Meaning: Hagall spoke of a challenge on the physical level. Jenny understood this to mean the physical challenge involved in organizing her mother's funeral, and that although times were hard at present, they would not last forever.

Daeg spoke of a light and Jenny realized that she had been emotionally in a very dark place since her mother's death. It also reminded her that her mother was now in the light and this gave her great comfort.

It showed Jenny the need for patience and the importance of allowing the grieving process to unfold, of using this time to look back over her life with her mother and to recognize all the lessons she had learnt from this.

Feoh showed Jenny that she needed to acknowledge the rich gifts of love and teaching that her mother had given her. It reminded her that no one can take her memories away from her. This reading proved a source of great strength and inspiration for Jenny during this difficult time in her life.

the world tree spread

This spread is designed to act as a guide to the next stage of your spiritual journey, giving knowledge about the next lesson you can learn, the next challenge ahead, your guides, allies and omens. It will speed you along your adventurous path towards new enlightenments, teaching you that everything that enters your life offers an opportunity for learning so that you can become a better, stronger and wiser person.

The World Tree

One of the oldest and most universal symbols in the world, images of a sacred tree appear among most earth-based belief systems and in such religions as Christianity and Kabbalism. In the Nordic tradition, Yggdrasil was the sacred ash tree of life and death. The roots of the tree are said to connect to the underworld, which is inhabited by many nature spirits, plant divas and elementals. By descending the tree while in a visionary state, the shaman could seek guidance and wisdom from these beings. The upper branches of the tree are said to ascend to the upper world, which is inhabited by angels, advanced souls and supernatural entities who are again sought out by the shaman on his visionary journeys. Some representations of the world tree also show the leaves and branches inhabited by discarnate souls on their way either to or from the earthly plane. The world tree is a powerful archetypal image and a source of great wisdom and knowledge.

Carving of Yggdrasil, the world tree.

Using Runes as an Oracle

The spread begins at the earth and rises up the trunk of the tree towards the heavens. It represents a phase of your spiritual journey, and this image should be clearly fixed in your mind when using the spread. You are not coming with a question or a problem, just an open heart, eager to learn how to make sure you progress on your path of learning. In this spread, the runes speak directly to you and for you. Listen to their wisdom.

Sample Reading

The positions have the following meanings:
1 What do you need to learn?
2 What will challenge you?
3 What is your guiding rune?
4 What power will help you?
5 What comes to warn you?
6 What do you need to let go of?
7 What will be the outcome of learning this lesson?

1 Nied: You need to learn that the past is just a memory and the future just a dream; the present is all you can influence.
2 Tyr reversed: You are challenged to look honestly at your weaknesses and resolve to turn them into strengths.
3 Peorth: Your guiding rune tells you to remember that you always have a choice in everything.
4 Feoh: The power behind you comes from the fact that you have a spiritual richness that is to be used for the benefit of all.
5 Hagall: You are warned that challenges are entering your life and that these are not to be feared, rather embraced.
6 Elhaz: You need to let go of fear for you have the power of protection within you.
7 Jara: This will lead to a time of reaping rewards for the seeds sown in the past.

advanced divination

These spreads are starting points to show you the range and flexibility of the runes. You can create your own spreads: as long as you maintain a strong intent, they will give you guidance about anything. Some spreads use many runes; either replace them between draws, having noted each one down, so that you always have 24 to draw from, or draw the runes as before, without replacing them. It is up to your intuition.

THE CELTIC CROSS SPREAD

1 What is the root of your lack of clarity?
2 How and where should you direct your energies?
3 What is blocking your progress?
4 What will help you overcome this blockage?
5 What are you still lacking?
6 What will be the outcome of this experience?

The Celtic cross, engraved with interlocking devices, represents the spirals of learning.

THOR'S HAMMER SPREAD

1 What mask do you show the world?
2 What fears are within you?
3 What are you seeking?
4 How should you best approach this?
5 What do you hope to become?
6 What is stopping you?
7 What is your destiny?
8 What do you need to learn to find your true self?
9 What is your true self?

Thor's hammer harnesses the energy of the Norse god of thunder.

Clarifying Unclear Answers

Sometimes after consulting the runes, things seem no clearer than they were before the reading, and you are left uncertain as to how to interpret them. The runes can occasionally be ambiguous, particularly if the question you are asking is not entirely straightforward. If this is the case, it may be necessary to draw an extra rune. This is done simply by asking the runes to provide a better explanation, and then drawing a single rune which should clarify the message the runes are trying to give.

rune magic

There is nothing mystical about magic. Magic comes from an understanding of the subtle vibrations that emanate from all things. Rune magic teaches how you can attune yourself to individual runes. As you work with the runes, they will teach you about the power of nature. By working with trees, colour, herbs and crystals, you will begin to understand more about your connection to and place in the universe.

Empowering Yourself

Nature teaches balance and harmony, for she is always seeking them. Whenever humanity upsets the natural balance of the world, nature quickly returns to a state of balance as soon as she is given the opportunity. Just visiting a disused quarry or railway line will show you the amazing power that nature has to reclaim and re-colonize the land.

Nature teaches by example and through vibrations, so regular communing with nature can be both enlightening and empowering. If you want to find your true connection and understand your full potential, spend as much time as you can among nature enjoying its beauty.

Wearing Runes

Another way to empower yourself is to wear a rune as a pendant around your neck. Runes emit powerful vibrations and by wearing a rune about your neck, you can subject the whole of your being to that positive vibration. This will have a strong protective effect and will also attract the qualities of the rune you are wearing into your life.

Meditate in a natural environment among plants and trees; they will teach and guide you if you are patient.

Healing Runes

Because of their harmonious vibrations, runes have strong and powerful healing properties. If you have a complaint or illness, you can ask for a healing rune to be revealed to you while holding your rune bag. Next, pick out a single rune and either hold it in your hand and meditate with it or place it upon the ailing area. You will be amazed at how apt the message of the rune is to your ailment, and it often gives you guidance on the root cause and best treatment. For instance, if you draw the Is rune, it will help you to remove blockages in the body and get things moving; it also teaches the importance of contemplation. Drawing the Lagu rune will empower you to release emotional issues and to find balance and harmony; it also teaches the importance of eating a balanced diet of natural foods. It is vital that you learn the lessons that each illness is trying to teach.

All the runes have their individual healing properties and lessons to teach, for they are intrinsically linked. Illness is your body's way of telling you that you are doing something that is causing disharmony or "dis-ease" to the body. Your body is trying to teach you a lesson and as the runes also teach lessons, it follows that each lesson can represent an aspect of return to "ease" or health.

Lay down, relax, then place a rune upon an ailing area of your body to give you guidance on your ailment.

using runes to help others

Once you have become familiar with the runes and the way they work, you can begin to help others, if you wish, by giving readings for them. Giving a reading for another person is the same as giving a reading for yourself, except that the other person draws the runes from your rune bag while you hold the clear intent in your mind of what each rune should represent.

Giving a Reading for Someone Else

Decide on a suitable spread for the runes by talking to the other person about the issue they wish to clarify. If, for example, you choose to use the three-rune spread, you would give the rune bag to the other person and ask them to draw out three runes, one at a time, and lay them on the casting cloth. As they draw out the first rune, you think, "I want this rune that they are drawing to comment upon the past". While they are drawing out the second rune, you think, "I want this rune that they are drawing to comment upon the present" and so on.

Once the person has drawn their runes, take your rune bag back into your possession so that the vibration of the remaining runes can help empower you with the reading. Allow your intuition to speak to you and take note of what it says. You can then tie these intuitive insights in with the meaning of each rune.

With all such work, the more you do it, the better you become. It is probably best to begin by giving readings to family and friends before venturing into the realm of giving "cold" readings to people you do not know well.

To heal someone, ask them to sit within their four chosen runes, facing the direction in which they feel most comfortable.

Healing Through the Four Elements

Healing others is an extension of the four-element spread. Once a patient has drawn the four runes and received their interpretation, ask the patient to sit facing the direction in which they feel most comfortable. Place the four runes in position; north, south, east and west as they appeared in the four-element spread. Make a note of the direction in which the patient chooses to face; this will give you an indication of where they are on their spiritual path. If they sit facing north, you know that they are mainly dealing with the physical. If they sit facing west they are trying to balance their emotional side. If they sit facing south they are looking towards their destiny and if they sit facing east, they are seeking wisdom. If they sit facing one of the cross points (north-east, south-east, south-west or north-west) this indicates that they are trying to integrate two areas into their life, seeking balance and harmony between them.

While the patient is sitting within the four runes, you may wish to beat a drum or sing a song. The vibrations from the music will help to amplify the healing vibrations of the runes. It is also good to get the patient to spend a few minutes at the end of the healing ceremony facing the opposite direction to their chosen one as this will help them to attract and integrate the energies of the other runes.

Once you are familiar with the runes, you can begin to help others by giving them readings.

runic wishing ceremony

If you write a wish in runic script and then burn the script in the flame of a fire or candle, your wish will be sent out into the universe and will draw all the energies towards you to make that wish come true. Such wishing ceremonies have been used for thousands of years and are extremely powerful. Wishes can be for anything as long as they are not selfish and do not come from the ego.

Making your Wish

Wishes can be written in runes as single words, for example "Love", "Health" or "Togetherness", or as letters requesting specific wishes, for example "I ask that (person's name) be able to grow in inspiration and beauty." Seal your wish with a rune; this can be done by drawing a single rune and writing it on the folded paper. As you watch your wish burn, visualize its energy travelling to every corner of the universe, sending a message that will attract all the right energies you need to make that wish come true.

Always remember that everything that comes to you throughout your journey in life comes to teach you, and is a stepping stone taking you closer to the realization of your wish.

1 Write a wish on a piece of paper using runic script. It can be in the form of a single word or may be a simple message. Seal the wish with a rune.

2 Cast the paper into the fire and, while it is burning, focus on the liberated energy of your wish travelling to every corner of the universe.

This Bindrune means "to gain inspiration".

Runes painted on a wand.

Runes carved on a staff.

Runes engraved on a sword.

TOOLS AND TALISMANS

As well as being worn about one's person as talismans, runes can also be painted, drawn or carved to empower magical tools. Traditionally, runes were inscribed on tools and weapons, typically on lance tips and sword blades, as protection and to guarantee victory in battle, and many archaeological finds of this kind have been made all over northern Europe.

If you have a staff, wand or other magical tool that you wish to empower, you can ask the runes to show you which runes you need and then draw out as many as your intuition dictates. These can then be burnt, carved or painted on to your tool.

Bindrunes

Bindrunes consist of two or more runes bound together into a single form to act as a magical power symbol. The meanings of the different elements are incorporated into the symbol to form a new and powerful energy. An example of a bindrune is shown here, but you can equally well create your own. All you need to do is to ask the runes to show you which ones to combine for your chosen purpose and then draw and combine as many runes as your intuition dictates.

runes and their meanings

There are many different varieties of runic writing, ranging from the Early or Elder Germanic script of 24 letters, to the Anglo-Saxon script with an original 28 letters rising to 33, and various Nordic, Danish and Swedish runic alphabets varying from 15 to 16 letters. Over 4,000 runic inscriptions and several runic manuscripts are still in existence, the vast majority of which originate from Sweden. Others are mainly found in Norway, Denmark, Britain and Iceland, and some have also been discovered on various islands off the coasts of Britain and Scandinavia, as well as in France, Germany and the former Soviet Union.

In the past, there were two main types of people who worked with the runes: runecutters, who had a limited knowledge of the runes and their protective qualities, and runemasters, both male and female, who had undergone many initiatory experiences to discover the deeper secrets of rune lore. These runemasters were held in the highest esteem. They knew not only how to divine successfully with runes, but also how to use runes to their advantage in magical and healing work.

Since the beginning of the 20th century, runes have been growing in popularity. Many books about runes are now available, and there are even schools teaching runic divination and the finer arts of rune lore. The fact that runes have lasted two whole millennia is an indication that their potential power has been undiminished by the years.

Rune lore is closely linked to the long spiritual history of the Scandinavians and their gods and goddesses, who are described in the ancient sagas. In Norse mythology, the chief god was Odin, the discoverer of the runes and the first runemaster. He was married to Frigg and they had two sons, Balder (the beautiful god) and Thor (the thunder god). Odin's brother, Loki, was the trickster god. Many other gods and goddesses are mentioned in the sagas, including Njord, the god of the sea, Freya, the goddess of war, love and magic, Idun, the goddess of healing and Tyr, the warrior god. The attributes of these deities are reflected in the meanings and magic of the runes.

Odin, the all-father of the Norse gods, experienced a shamanic initiation, during which time the runes appeared to him. Legend tells that he hanged himself upside down on the great ash tree Yggdrasil, the World Tree or Tree of Life. After nine days and nights, Odin died on the tree, but was reborn through his unquenchable will, bringing back with him to the world the knowledge and wisdom of the world beyond – and the runes – as a gift to humankind.

feoh ᚠ

Meaning: Cattle

To the Nordic people, cattle were a sign of status and wealth. Like all animals, cattle were sacred but they were also killed and their meat feasted upon at times of celebration, showing that wealth should be used for the benefit of all. While physical wealth is transient, spiritual wealth is permanent and can never be taken away from you, no matter how many times you share your wisdom. If you are unaware of your gifts it does not mean that you have none; on the contrary, it means that you have not yet uncovered them. Each person has many gifts; once they are recognized, they can be used.

Interpretation of Rune

"Wealth should never be hoarded but used for the benefit of all."
Feoh speaks of a spiritual richness that is to be used for the benefit of all. Let your unselfish abundance shine forth to lighten your path and the paths of others. It will never run out but you should not waste it on those who will abuse it.

Interpretation of Reversed Rune

You have great richness within you, but its light is masked by emotional imbalances. Strive for balance in your life and you will discover the rich wealth of gifts and talents that are already yours. Claim your destiny.

FEOH
Corresponding letter: F
Rune: ᚠ
Meaning: Cattle
Divinatory meaning:
Spiritual richness

Associations
Tree: Elder
Colour: Light red
Herb: Nettle
Gemstone: Moss agate

---

ur ᚢ

Meaning: Auroch

Aurochs were wild oxen and a powerful totem of Nordic tradition symbolizing strength. Nowadays, many people equate strength with dominance and inflexibility. They also confuse pride with strength, whereas pride is actually a weakness created by the ego. To find your true strength, you must first face your weaknesses. You can then turn them into strengths. This process can be frightening for many people.

Interpretation of Rune

"To find your true strength, you must first face your weaknesses."
You have the strength within you to fulfil all your dreams, but with that strength comes responsibility. It should not be used to exert power over others, but to stop others exerting power over you. Use it to keep you focused on your path. Some people are always negative. Strength comes from not letting them upset you and this in turn comes from mastering the ego.

Interpretation of Reversed Rune

To be strong, you must first know weakness. Look honestly within yourself without fear, knowing that once you recognize those areas of weakness, you will be able to work on them to turn them into strengths.

UR
Corresponding letter: U
Rune: ᚢ
Meaning: Auroch
Divinatory meaning:
Strength

Associations
Tree: Birch
Colour: Dark green
Herb: Sphagnum moss
Gemstone: Carbuncle

thorn ᚦ

Meaning: Thorn

The shamans and magicians of northern Europe have long associated thorn trees with spiritual authority. Blackthorn was greatly favoured as the material for making staffs and powerful wands. Thorn trees are symbolic of protection and their wood was often used to make talismans to ward off evil. The protection that comes from the thorn tree is the protection of spiritual authority, and gives you the power to stand up for the truth when surrounded by lies, and to claim the spiritual path that is your birthright. The blackthorn has a sister tree, the hawthorn, which, while being a powerful protective tree like the blackthorn, also has soothing and balancing feminine energies.

Interpretation of Rune

"You have the power to face anything that might cross your path."
Fear nothing, for you have the authority to claim your destiny. Let no one deter you from your search for the truth. Hold fast to your birthright, be a spiritual being, but always remember to keep your feet firmly on the ground. Spiritual authority brings power and it is up to you to use that power in an unselfish and loving way. Power can corrupt if you do not have a true and honest heart. You should never need to tell others of your authority; knowing that you have it should be enough. To utilize the power of this rune fully, you must first master the ego.

THORN
Corresponding letter: Th
Rune: ᚦ
Meaning: Thorn
Divinatory meaning:
Spiritual authority

Associations
Tree: Thorn/oak
Colour: Bright red
Herb: Houseleek
Gemstone: Sapphire

---

ansur ᚫ

Meaning: Mouth

In the Nordic tradition, the mouth is symbolic of communication. Messages come in many forms and communication problems arise from an inability to decipher these messages correctly. A word can have completely different meanings to different people. For instance, to someone brought up in northern Europe, the word "seaside" creates a picture of sand, seaweed and cold sea, while to someone brought up in the Caribbean it creates a picture of palm trees, blue water and scorching sun.

Interpretation of Rune

"Everything that comes to you comes to teach you."
The answers to your questions are already here: you have just not heard them yet. Look for signs and confirmations which are all around you. Everything has significance. If you learn this truth, you will understand the messages around you. Check that you are not ignoring the message because you do not like its contents. Trust that everything comes to teach you, and that by acknowledging the truth you will grow in wisdom.

Interpretation of Reversed Rune

You have not found answers because you are asking the wrong questions. Seek in a different way; look within and all will be clear.

ANSUR
Corresponding letter: A
Rune: ᚫ
Meaning: Mouth
Divinatory meaning:
Message

Associations
Tree: Ash
Colour: Dark blue
Herb: Fly agaric
Gemstone: Emerald

rad ᚱ

Meaning: Cartwheel

Life is a journey along which we encounter challenges. Everything in life is cyclical. Once you recognize this fact, you can "go with the flow" and let things unfold rather than always resisting. When times are difficult, be assured that they will not go on forever. Once you have learnt the lessons that the hard times are trying to teach you, you will no longer need to suffer them. The faster you learn, the faster you will progress, so embrace everything with pleasure, knowing that there are lessons to be learnt.

Interpretation of Rune

"When times are difficult, be sure that they will not go on forever."
Recognize that everything comes in cycles and that by following these cycles, you will be able to progress quickly and efficiently. Align yourself to the seasons by eating seasonal foods and honouring the turning of the year. Embrace hard times in the certainty that the harder it is now, the more beautiful things will be in the future. Everything has its opposite, and challenges bring equal and opposite rewards.

Interpretation of Reversed Rune

Stop trying to resist the inevitable. Your path is set out before you; tread it without fear. Take one step at a time and you will soon find yourself "flowing" once more.

RAD
Corresponding letter: R
Rune: ᚱ
Meaning: Cartwheel
Divinatory meaning:
Wheel of life

Associations
Tree: Oak
Colour: Bright red
Herb: Mugwort
Gemstone: Chrysoprase

ken ᚲ

Meaning: Torch

Illumination allows you to see in the dark. Enlightenment is a spiritual illumination. It is coming into a new understanding, like opening your eyes for the first time or like turning on a light. You are not seeing anything new, you are just seeing it for the first time. Enlightenment is a beginning, not an end. This new understanding needs to be utilized and tempered with wisdom before its true worth and power can be known. With knowledge comes responsibility: it is vital that you use your knowledge and power only for what is good and right.

Interpretation of Rune

"Enlightenment needs to be tempered with wisdom before its true worth and power can be known."
You are coming into a new understanding of life and its meaning. New insights await you but this is not a time for complacency. You must use this new understanding or it will be worthless to you. Always look for ways in which you can use your insights for the good of yourself and others. Enlightenment is like a jug of fine wine: it must be poured out before it can be refilled. Do not be fooled into thinking that enlightenment is your goal in life. It is only the starting point of an adventure of learning that will show you great wisdom and understanding.

KEN
Corresponding letter: K
Rune: ᚲ
Meaning: Torch
Divinatory meaning:
Enlightenment

Associations
Tree: Pine
Colour: Light red
Herb: Cowslip
Gemstone: Bloodstone

geofu X

Meaning: Gift

To receive a gift, you must also be a giver. Likewise, if you give, you must be willing to receive. The cycle of giving and receiving must never be broken. Those who take without giving on a physical or emotional level lose their own spiritual gifts. To tread a spiritual path, you must also be both a giver and a receiver. To be truly balanced you must be able to receive a gift with total humility, knowing that if you abuse a spiritual gift, you will lose it. Compassion is a sharing of the gift of love and understanding. Encouragement is the sharing of the gift of empowerment. Each person has many gifts; once they are recognized, they can be used for the good of all.

Interpretation of Rune

"To tread a spiritual path, you must be both giver and receiver."
A gift is coming to you and this presents you with a choice. You can either accept it or reject it. If you choose to accept it, you must be prepared to give in return. Everything has its price, but with spiritual gifts the cost is always worth it in the end. You must find the balance between giving and receiving and learn the lesson of responsible giving. You must learn when to give and who to give to. It is not appropriate to give to everyone for there are those who do not wish to receive, so giving to them is a waste of energy and an abuse of your own gifts.

GEOFU
Corresponding letter: G
Rune: X
Meaning: Gift
Divinatory meaning:
Spiritual gift

Associations
Tree: Ash/elm
Colour: Deep blue
Herb: Heartsease
Gemstone: Opal

wynn ᚹ

Meaning: Happiness

True happiness only comes to those who are balanced. Happiness is found within and is not dependent on any other person or thing. You must be at peace with your place in life. This requires you to eat, think and act in a balanced manner. Healthy eating (fresh, natural, organic, unrefined foods) is fundamental and will naturally lead to healthy thoughts and actions. So seek balance and harmony within, and you will attract peace and happiness for yourself. Happiness comes from seeking and finding the truth, then integrating it into every aspect of your life.

Interpretation of Rune

"To have happiness, you must be at peace with yourself."
Happiness is yours if you are willing to work for it. You must strive for balance and harmony. Always be looking for solutions rather than dwelling upon problems. For happiness to last, it needs to be founded upon truth and honesty. Seek only what is good and right, and good fortune cannot fail to follow.

Interpretation of Reversed Rune

The happiness you seek is already yours, but your attachment to the past is preventing you from seeing it. It is time to let go of the old and embrace the new.

WYNN
Corresponding letter: W
Rune: ᚹ
Meaning: Happiness
Divinatory meaning:
Balance

Associations
Tree: Ash
Colour: Yellow
Herb: Flax
Gemstone: Diamond

hagall ᚺ

Meaning: Hail

Challenges occur to teach you. When you have a vision of how you would like your future to be, you send energy as thought waves out into the universe. These vibrations attract to you all the things that need to be in place before that dream can become reality. You cannot know all the lessons, but if you stay fixed on your dream, be assured that you will be attracting all the lessons you need. When life becomes difficult, it is not a sign to abandon your dream, it is merely a stepping stone to the realization of that dream. It is an opportunity to learn lessons that you will need when your dream becomes reality. Face the challenge – when you have overcome it, you will be stronger and wiser.

Interpretation of Rune

"Never shy away from challenges as they strengthen and teach you throughout your life."

Challenges are occurring in your life. These are not to be feared, but to be embraced. A hailstorm may seem daunting, but if you catch a hailstone you will realize that it is only water. So it is with challenges. Grit your teeth, fire up your determination, and face the challenges head-on in the assurance that they are just stepping stones to the realization of your dream. Every challenge comes to teach. Remember, the greater the challenge, potentially the more wisdom you can acquire.

HAGALL
Corresponding letter: H
Rune: ᚺ
Meaning: Hail
Divinatory meaning: Challenge

Associations
Tree: Ash/yew
Colour: Light blue
Herb: Lily-of-the-valley
Gemstone: Onyx

nied ᚾ

Meaning: Need

What we want and what we need in our lives are often completely different. If you want to be strong, you will need to examine your weaknesses. This creates a paradox. It is only when you realize that the weaknesses need to be faced and turned to strengths, that you will begin to understand the difference between wants and needs. To be strong, you must first experience weakness; to find your path, you must first lose it; to be beautiful within, you must first face up to your ugly inner side.

Interpretation of Rune

"To achieve your wants, you often need to experience the very opposite of your wants."

You are getting exactly what you need at this moment to allow you to make the best progress on your spiritual path. It may appear to be the very opposite of what you want, but this state is merely a series of lessons that must be learnt so that you can make the transition from negative to positive. You need to have total acceptance of the past, to keep your mind fixed on where you want to be, while trusting that everything in the present is meant to be there and is to be learnt from. The past is just a memory, the future just a dream; the present is the only place where you can have influence.

NIED
Corresponding letter: N
Rune: ᚾ
Meaning: Need
Divinatory meaning: Need

Associations
Tree: Beech
Colour: Black
Herb: Bistort
Gemstone: Lapis lazuli

is \

Meaning: Ice
Ice can form an impenetrable barrier. The only thing you can do is wait for the thaw. But winter is not a time for idleness. Although nothing appears to be moving, everything must be in place and ready if you are to take full advantage of the coming thaw. Winter is also a time of contemplation, a time to assimilate all the lessons that the past has taught, to look to the future and reaffirm your dreams. Recognize that the time you are in is just another phase of your unfolding path of learning; when this phase is over, a new one will begin. Use this time to rest a while; you will need to focus all your energies for what is to come.

Interpretation of Rune
"When life seems at a standstill, review the past and look ahead."
Things appear to be at a standstill and this is not a time to try to force movement. Patience and wisdom are called for: patience because you will have to wait until things change externally before you can proceed; and wisdom because you need to decide how best to use your waiting time. This is not the time to be abandoning your dreams; on the contrary, this is an opportunity for you to reaffirm them. This is a time for contemplation and preparation, not for depression and regrets. Be assured that things will change as surely as winter changes to spring and spring to summer.

IS
Corresponding letter: I
Rune: \
Meaning: Ice
Divinatory meaning: Standstill

Associations
Tree: Alder
Colour: Black
Herb: Henbane
Gemstone: Cat's-eye

jara ᛃ

Meaning: Harvest
Harvest is the time of hardest work. The fruits of your labour must be collected and stored if they are not to spoil. If the winter is to be survived, it is imperative that as much grain and produce as possible is stored. Everything must be done correctly. If grains are not stored in the right way, they will rot and spoil long before the winter is over. This is certainly not a time to be resting on your laurels. The harvest feasting takes place only after the harvest is finished. You are at the end of a cycle, but remember that endings only lead to new beginnings.

Interpretation of Rune
"A time of hard work, and of reaping rewards for past efforts."
This is a time of plenty, a time of joy and celebration. But it is also a time of great work with no time for complacency. The harvest does not last forever. The winter of more hard lessons lies ahead and you would do well to make sure that you have stored enough knowledge and wisdom to face your next challenges. This is another turning point in your life, not your goal. There are greater harvests for you to experience in the future, but before any harvest there has to be preparation of the land, sowing of the seed, tending of the seedlings and support of the forming life-giving fruits.

JARA
Corresponding letter: J
Rune: ᛃ
Meaning: Harvest
Divinatory meaning: Harvest

Associations
Tree: Oak
Colour: Light blue
Herb: Rosemary
Gemstone: Cornelian

eoh ᛇ

Meaning: Yew Tree

The yew tree has a long association with immortality and the cycle of death and rebirth. As a yew tree grows, its central trunk becomes soft and starts to decay. While this occurs, a new sapling begins to grow within the tree. When the tree matures, the same process continues to occur until the tree is made up of many trees growing from the centre outwards. This amazing regeneration is what enables a yew tree to grow to an immense size and age. A yew tree is said to have known many lives and so can help you remember past lives. Because of its longevity, the yew is also an ancient wisdom-keeper.

Interpretation of Rune

"By embracing change, you will make quick progress along your spiritual path."

This is a time of transformation; a time to let go of the old and embrace the new. It is a time of death, the dying of the past, and yet it is also a time of new beginnings, new life and new dreams. The only constant is change, and if you want to make quick and efficient progress on your path, you have to learn to embrace change instead of resisting it. To resist change is to risk stagnation. Do not be afraid; change is scary, but if you remain true to yourself and keep to your path, you will soon find yourself basking in the fresh sun of new enlightenments.

EOH
Corresponding letter: Y
Rune: ᛇ
Meaning: Yew tree
Divinatory meaning:
Transformation

Associations
Tree: Yew
Colour: Dark blue
Herb: Mandrake
Gemstone: Topaz

---

peorth ᛈ

Meaning: Dice Cup

The dice cup is the source of chance or fate. A die which is not thrown is just a lump of wood with dots on it. It is only when it is thrown that it has significance. It is in the hands of fate. People think of fate as an inevitable tide, but it merely presents you with choices. There is the choice of whether or not to throw the dice and whether to heed what the dice say. Life is full of choices, but many people choose to let the hand of fate guide them instead of taking charge of their own destiny.

Interpretation of Rune

"Make your own choices and take charge of your own destiny."

You always have a choice in everything. No one can upset you, instead you can only choose to be upset. No one can exert power over you unless you choose to allow them to. Do not allow others to compromise your truth and do not let others prevent you from doing what you need to do. The only danger here is not to make a choice, to leave things to fate.

Interpretation of Reversed Rune

The dice have been rolled and fate has control of your life, but it does not have to be this way. You can regain power. Start to make choices for yourself instead of following the choices of others.

PEORTH
Corresponding letter: P
Rune: ᛈ
Meaning: Dice cup
Divinatory meaning:
Choice

Associations
Tree: Beech
Colour: Black
Herb: Aconite
Gemstone: Aquamarine

elhaz ᛉ

Meaning: Elk

To the Nordic people, the elk was a powerful totemic animal with very strong protective energies. This rune is said to guard the wearer against all attacks and dangers, both physical and psychic. The rune represents the elk when the animal is viewed face on. Its antlers were thought of as psychic receivers which could pick up the subtle vibrations of living things. The protective energies of the elk come not only from its ability to sense danger, but also its speed and the skill with which it flees dangerous situations. Therefore, the Elhaz rune is a powerful ally to help you to find a safe passage through difficult times.

Interpretation of Rune
"Although your path is fraught with danger, you have the power of protection within you."
You will be safe as long as you do not act recklessly. This is a favourable time for risky ventures, although all things must be built on firm foundations. Do not become complacent.

Interpretation of Reversed Rune
Proceed with caution and do not act in haste. In your present situation you are vulnerable to hostile influences and need to concentrate on building your strength physically, emotionally and spiritually before pressing forwards.

ELHAZ
Corresponding letter: Z
Rune: ᛉ
Meaning: Elk
Divinatory meaning: Protection

Associations
Tree: Yew
Colour: Gold
Herb: Angelica
Gemstone: Amethyst

sigel ᛋ

Meaning: The Sun

To the Nordic people, the sun was considered the giver of life, for without its rays there would be no food and sustenance. The sun is associated with all that is good, just and right. The light of the sun banishes darkness and rejuvenates the spirit. It is also the "destroyer of ice", as one Icelandic runic poem describes it, and is therefore a powerful rune to counteract the negative aspects of the Is rune, which means ice and is interpreted as being at a standstill. Sigel is also a rune of truth; the power of light illuminates the darkness of deception, giving clarity of thought and vision. It will show you not only deception in others, but within you. It will shine a light upon the path of all who hold it.

Interpretation of Rune
"You have the power to bring things to fruition."
You have the power to bring things to fruition. Good fortune awaits you and there is a positive feel to everything in your life. This is not a time to rest and relax, however, rather it is an ideal time to look within at the darker aspects of your nature. The power of the sun will enable you to face those dark parts of your being squarely without fear and finally to gain power over them. This is a good time to seek solutions to problems as they are all within your grasp.

SIGEL
Corresponding letter: S
Rune: ᛋ
Meaning: The sun
Divinatory meaning: Good fortune

Associations
Tree: Juniper
Colour: White/silver
Herb: Mistletoe
Gemstone: Ruby

tyr ↑

Meaning: Tyr (the Warrior God)

The path of the warrior presents challenges and initiations. He must be of a good and strong heart, with a firm belief in the sacredness of that which he protects. As a companion, one could not wish for a better ally, for the warrior has a natural instinct to protect and survive. He is always resourceful and focuses on solutions rather than problems. The wise warrior knows that mistakes are not failures, but rather lessons to be learnt if one is honest and humble enough to seek. The man who makes no mistakes in his life becomes an old fool.

Interpretation of Rune

"Now is the time to make use of all the skills and wisdom that you have learnt so far."
This rune symbolizes new challenges and initiations into new understandings. There is a need for fearlessness, for your victory is assured if your heart remains true. Protect your faith, as it will be challenged, but the truth will always be victorious in the end.

Interpretation of Reversed Rune

You have all the powers you need for the challenges ahead but you need to unlock your true potential. Look honestly at your weaknesses and resolve to turn them into strengths. The warrior is within you and it is now time to let that energy come forth.

TYR
Corresponding letter: T
Rune: ↑
Meaning: Warrior god
Divinatory meaning:
Initiation

Associations
Tree: Oak
Colour: Bright red
Herb: Sage
Gemstone: Coral

beorc ᛒ

Meaning: Birch Tree

The birch tree is a pioneer tree. When forest or scrubland is destroyed by fire, the birch is one of the first trees to re-colonize the land. It is symbolic of birth and new beginnings, like the phoenix rising from the ashes. Magically, the birch tree has long been associated with purification. The birch broom was used to sweep negativity from a house, while the punishment of "birching" was said to drive evil from criminals. The old pagan ritual of beating the bounds to mark land boundaries and to cleanse negativity from the soil also utilized birch.

Interpretation of Rune

"This is an exciting time of new beginnings and fresh adventures."
This is a time of great activity and energy. This is a time to sow seeds, but remember that the harvest is still a long way off; do not expect to see immediate rewards for your efforts, as new ideas need nurturing and feeding before they will bear fruit. This is a time to make sure that the past is truly put in its place. If one has learnt all the lessons that the past has had to teach, it need never be revisited. It can be left behind and you can venture forth with boldness to embrace new pastures. This is also a good time to think about a spiritual spring cleaning, clearing away the old to make way for the new.

BEORC
Corresponding letter: B
Rune: ᛒ
Meaning: Birch tree
Divinatory meaning:
New beginnings

Associations
Tree: Birch
Colour: Dark green
Herb: Lady's mantle
Gemstone: Moonstone

ehwaz ᛗ

Meaning: Horse
The horse was regarded as a sacred animal throughout the old world and is recorded in many myths and legends as a faithful and loyal ally. Its energy is powerful and primal, helping you to avoid obstacles and to make swift progress along your path. The horse is also associated with fire, the element of free expression and unfolding destiny. The energy of the horse can help to clear stagnation and remove blocks. This makes it a valuable ally on the spiritual path because the only constant is change.

Interpretation of Rune
"Always be as loyal to those around you as they are to you."
You have the support to be able to make swift progress along your path, but this is dependent upon you being as loyal and supportive to those around you as they are to you. The horse is a proud animal but it does not let its pride get in the way of its purpose. In the same way, you should always be proud of your achievements while remaining outwardly humble.

Interpretation of Reversed Rune
You need to make new connections. This will draw the energies towards you that will help you overcome all obstacles. Seek out those who share your attitude, knowing that everyone who enters your life has lessons to teach you.

EHWAZ
Corresponding letter: E
Rune: ᛗ
Meaning: Horse
Divinatory meaning: Progress

Associations
Tree: Oak/ash
Colour: White
Herb: Ragwort
Gemstone: Iceland spar

---

mann ᛗ

Meaning: Human Being
Every human being has a destiny and it is their right to fulfil it. Destiny is all about choice. You can choose to take responsibility for your life, to be a spiritual being, or you can choose to drift along with whatever life throws at you. The path of destiny is not easy, for it holds many lessons and challenges along the way, but it is a path of growth and fulfilment. The other path appears easier, but it is filled with ill-health and dissatisfaction.

Interpretation of Rune
"The path of destiny is a path of growth and fulfilment."
Your destiny awaits you, so claim it. For you to be a spiritual being, you must be balanced in body, mind and spirit. Embrace everything – good and bad – with total acceptance and pleasure. By learning each lesson as it presents itself, you will go onwards and upwards.

Interpretation of Reversed Rune
The path of destiny seems hard, but as you tread it, you become wiser and stronger. Have faith – you have the strength and power to deal with all of life's problems and to make choices as long as you are willing to learn. Do not let your own ego, or those of others, fill your mind with misgivings.

MANN
Corresponding letter: M
Rune: ᛗ
Meaning: Human being
Divinatory meaning: Destiny

Associations
Tree: Holly
Colour: Deep red
Herb: Madder
Gemstone: Garnet

lagu ᛚ

Meaning: Water, Sea

Water is a primal power that can never be truly contained or controlled. All water flows where it will, drawn back and forth by the power of the moon. This includes the sea, the fluid within plants and the fluids within you. To be in harmony with creation, you need to attune yourself to the seasons and the moon. Eating and living in harmony with nature around you gives you a new perspective and opens up many possibilities to acquire new and greater knowledge and transform it into wisdom.

Interpretation of Rune

"Being in harmony with creation gives you emotional balance."
It is only by attunement to creation that your life will truly flow as it is meant to. Emotional balance comes from eating in balance with creation around you. Natural foods lead to natural flow, whereas unnatural foods lead to disharmony and stagnation. The sea is always fluid and moving, so it should be a part of your life. Embrace change, for it is the only constant.

Interpretation of Reversed Rune

You need to learn to go with the flow. There is a need to initiate some movement into many areas of your life, otherwise you will start to become stagnant. A few simple changes can bring about great, positive effects.

LAGU
Corresponding letter: L
Rune: ᛚ
Meaning: Water, sea
Divinatory meaning:
Attunement to creation

Associations
Tree: Willow
Colour: Deep green
Herb: Leek
Gemstone: Pearl

---

ing ᛜ

Meaning: Ing (the Fertility God)

Ing symbolizes the spark of creation, the power to give life and to make the land fertile. It is the fire within everyone that drives them forwards and keeps them striving towards spiritual fulfilment; it is the power to keep going when things get tough. This fire can lie dormant for many years, but when it is fuelled by the breath of acknowledgement, by its existence being recognized, it is almost impossible to extinguish. Ing teaches that you cannot change the past; the present is the only place where you can truly have influence. Ing helps you to let the past go, and keeps your eyes on your dream for the future, while you live and work in the here and now.

Interpretation of Rune

"The fire of inspiration urges you to strive for spiritual fulfilment."
You are on a spiritual path and although you may feel isolated at times, you can be safe in the knowledge that within you burns the fire of inspiration which urges you ever onwards and upwards. Feed the fire by always striving to learn more, never resting in the illusion of complacency. Seek only answers and never become waylaid with too many questions. Live one day at a time, knowing that the past is just a memory, the future just a dream, and the here and now is what matters.

ING
Corresponding letter: ng
Rune: ᛜ
Meaning: The fertility god
Divinatory meaning:
Fire within

Associations:
Tree: Apple
Colour: Yellow
Herb: Self-heal
Gemstone: Amber

daeg ᛞ

Meaning: Day (Light)

Daeg is the rune of midday and midsummer. It represents the positive energy of light at its most potent and powerful and is therefore a rune of great protection when painted over doorways and on window shutters. Daeg is positivity at its strongest, signifying success, growth, progress, clarity of vision and protection against harmful influences. It allows you to see the positive within every negative. Daeg also helps you remember that everything in life is given to you. If you do not use these gifts with love and beauty, they will be taken from you. You own nothing; everything is lent to you by the creator, so always use your gifts with respect and wisdom.

Interpretation of Rune

"While you remain true, only good fortune can come your way."
The power of the light shines before you, guiding you clearly upon your path, as long as you remain true. You need have no fear, for you are well protected by the power of the light. The light will give you clear vision so that you may see and avoid dangers before they enter your life. The only warning is against being blinded, although it is not the light that will blind you, but your ego. The ego, if not mastered, will allow your success to blind you, so always remain humble and thankful for all the good things that come to you.

DAEG
Corresponding letter: D
Rune: ᛞ
Meaning: Day (light)
Divinatory meaning: Light

Associations
Tree: Spruce
Colour: Light blue
Herb: Clary
Gemstone: Diamond

othel ᛟ

Meaning: Possession

Othel is the rune into which energies can be concentrated and focused. It has an image of an enclosure of land or of a magical circle. Although Othel means "a possession", it is in the sense of holding rather than owning. We own nothing; all things are merely loaned to us, including our bodies. For the power of Othel to be experienced, you need to be able to concentrate and relax at the same time. Focus on a thought, then wait patiently for other energies to be attracted to it. Never try to force things, but always keep in mind where you want to go.

Interpretation of Rune

"Focus your thoughts to attract the right energies that you need to make your dream reality."
This is a time to re-focus. Concentration is needed if you are to read all the signs that are appearing before you. Do not try to force issues. Your dream is like a dove sitting in your hand. If you try to possess it or to keep hold of it, you risk killing it.

Interpretation of Reversed Rune

If you try to own something, you will risk losing it. Allow everything and everyone to be. If you do not like something, you can only change by initiating change within yourself.

OTHEL
Corresponding letter: O
Rune: ᛟ
Meaning: Possession
Divinatory meaning: Focus and freedom

Associations
Tree: Hawthorn
Colour: Deep yellow
Herb: Clover
Gemstone: Ruby

Index

a
Aces, 15, 33
  of Cups, 28
  of Pentacles, 26
  of Swords, 22
  of Wands, 24
aetts, 71
Air element, 14, 15, 70, 74, 74
alphabets, runic, 11, 71, 81
angelica flowers, 68
angels, 75
Anglo-Saxon script, 81
Ansur rune, 83
Anubis, 21
apple, and rune-making, 70
Aquarius, 20
Aries, 17
ash tree, 70, 75
astrology, 14
aura, 44, 45

b
Balder, 81
Beorc rune, 70, 90
bindrunes, 79
birch, 70, 90
blackthorn, 70, 83
"Book of Changes" see I Ching
breathing, 44, 72

c
Cancer, 17, 21
candles, 44, 45, 71
Capricorn, 20
cardinal directions (I Ching), 41
casting cloth, 69, 71
Celtic Cross spread (runes), 76
Celtic Cross spread (Tarot), 34-5
Celts, 68, 70
Chariot (in Major Arcana), 17, 33
Chên (in I Ching), 43, 46, 47, 62
Chi Chi (in I Ching), 65
Chia Jên (in I Ching), 59
Chieh (in I Ching), 45, 64
Chien (in I Ching), 63
Ch'ien (in I Ching), 53
Chien (in I Ching), 59
Chi'en (in I Ching), 43, 46, 47, 50
Chin (in I Ching), 58
Chinese philosophy, 9, 40
Ching (in I Ching), 61
Chou, Duke of, 42, 49
Chou Hsin, Emperor, 42
Christianity, 75
Chun (in I Ching), 50
Chung Fu (in I Ching), 65
Clubs, 14, 24
colour, and runes, 11, 68, 77
Confucius, 41, 42
corn offering, 70
"Courtship Card", 29
creation, 40, 41, 42
Crusaders, 8
crystals, and runes, 11, 68, 70, 77
"Cup of Life", 28
Cups (in Minor Arcana), 14, 15, 28-9

d
Daeg rune, 74, 93
Day of Judgement, 21
Death (in Major Arcana), 19, 33, 35
Devil (in Major Arcana), 20, 33
Diamonds, 14, 26
drumming, 78

e
Early Germanic alphabet, 71, 81
Early Heaven Arrangement (Pa Kua), 40, 42
Earth element, 14, 15, 70, 74, 74
Egyptians, ancient, 8
Ehwaz rune, 91
Eight, 15, 33
  of Cups, 29, 35
  of Pentacles, 27
  of Swords, 23
  of Wands, 25
Elder Futhark alphabet, 71, 81
elementals, 75
elements, four, 14, 15, 70, 74, 78
Elhaz rune, 68, 75, 89
Emperor (in Major Arcana), 17, 33
empowerment, 67, 77
Empress (in Major Arcana), 17, 33
enlightenment, 84
Eoh rune, 70, 73, 73, 88

f
Female Pope see High Priestess
Fêng [in I Ching], 63
Feoh rune, 74, 75, 82
Fire element, 14, 15, 70, 74, 74
Five, 33
  of Cups, 28
  of Pentacles, 26
  of Swords, 22, 35
  of Wands, 24
"Five Confucian Classics", 42
Fool (in Major Arcana), 14, 15, 16, 33
Four, 33
  of Cups, 28
  of Pentacles, 26
  of Swords, 22, 35
  of Wands, 24
four-element spread (runes), 74, 78
Freya, 81
Frigg, 81
Fu (in I Ching), 55
Fu Hsi, Emperor, 40, 42, 42

g
Gemini, 17
Geofu rune, 73, 73, 85
Germanic tribes, 68
Gypsy spread see Romany spread

h
Hagall rune, 74, 75, 86
Hanged Man (in Major Arcana), 10, 19, 33, 35
hawthorn, 70, 83
hazel, and rune-making, 70
healing, and runes, 11, 67, 77, 78, 78
Hearts, 14, 28
Hêng (in I Ching), 57
herbs, and runes, 11, 68, 77
Hercules, 19
Hermit (in Major Arcana), 18, 33, 35, 37
hexagrams (in I Ching), 9, 40, 42, 43, 47
  commentaries on the 64 hexagrams, 49, 50-65
  constructing a hexagram, 45
  the first line, 49
  the second line, 49
  the third line, 49
  the fourth line, 49
  the fifth line, 49
  table of, 46
Hierophant (in Major Arcana), 17, 33
High Priestess (in Major Arcana), 16, 17, 33, 35
higher self, 44, 72
"Holy Grail", 28
Hsiao Ch'u (in I Ching), 52
Hsiao Kuo (in I Ching), 65
Hsieh (in I Ching), 59
Hsien (in I Ching), 57
Hsu (in I Ching), 51
Huan (in I Ching), 64

i
I Ching, 8
  based on hexagrams, 9
  a blueprint for the universe, 39, 42
  the cardinal directions, 41
  "changing" lines, 10
  consulting the oracle, 44-5
  changing lines, 45
  constructing a hexagram, 45
  formulating a question, 44, 49
  interpretation, 49
  ritual, 44
  gradations of yin and yang, 41
  hexagrams, 9, 40, 42, 43, 45, 46
  later history, 42
  and meditation, 10
  origin, 9, 39, 40
  the Pa Kua, 40, 41, 42, 49
  and ritual, 10, 44
  trigrams, 40-43, 47
  the unifying principle, 40
  yin and yang, 10, 40
I (in I Ching), 45, 56, 60
Idun, 81
incense burning, 44, 71
Ing rune, 92
intuition
  and I Ching, 44
  and runes, 11, 71, 72, 79
  and Tarot, 9, 13
Is rune, 74, 87
Isis, 16

j
Jara rune, 75, 87
Judgement (in Major Arcana), 21, 33

Jung, Carl, 42
Jupiter, 18
Justice (in Major Arcana), 15, 18, 33

k

Kabbalism, 75
K'an (in I Ching), 43, 46, 47, 57
Kên (in I Ching), 43, 46, 47, 62
Ken rune, 84
King, 14, 15
　of Cups, 29, 35
　of Pentacles, 27
　of Swords, 23
　of Wands, 25
　Knights, 14, 15
　of Cups, 29
　of Pentacles, 27
　of Swords, 23
　of Wands, 25
Ko (in I Ching), 62
Kou (in I Ching), 60
Ku (in I Ching), 54
kua, 40
Kuai (in I Ching), 60
Kuan (in I Ching), 54
K'uei (in I Ching), 59
Kueu Mei (in I Ching), 63
K'un (in I Ching), 61
K'un (in I Ching), 43, 46, 47, 50

l

Lagu rune, 77, 92
Later Heaven Arrangement (Pa Kua), 40
Leo, 19
Li (in I Ching), 43, 46, 47, 57
Libra, 18
Lin (in I Ching), 54
Loki, 81
Lovers (in Major Arcana), 17, 33
Lu (in I Ching), 52, 63

m

magic
　and runes, 77, 83
　and symbols, 7
　tools, 79
Magician (in Major Arcana), 16, 33
Major Arcana, 8, 13
　first group (the material world), 14, 16-17
　second group (the intuitive mind), 14, 18-19
　third group (the realm of change), 14, 20-21
　the Fool, 14, 15, 16
　quick guide, 33
Mann rune, 91
Mars, 20
meditation
　and I Ching, 10, 56
　and runes, 10, 11, 68, 68, 72, 77, 77
Memphis, Egypt, 8
Mêng (in I Ching), 50
Mercury, 16
Ming I (in I Ching), 58
Minor Arcana, 8, 13, 14
　Cups, 14, 15, 28-9
　Pentacles, 14, 15, 26-7
　Swords, 14, 15, 22-3
　Wands, 14, 15, 24-5
　quick guide, 33
Moon, and the Major Arcana, 14, 16, 21, 33

n

Native Americans, 70
nature, and runes, 77
Nemean lion, 19
Neptune, 19
Nied rune, 75, 86
Nine, 33
　of Cups, 29
　of Pentacles, 27
　of Swords, 23
　of Wands, 25
Njord, 81
Nordic people, 70, 82, 89
Nordic tradition, 74, 75, 82, 83
Norse mythology, 10, 81

o

oak, and rune-making, 70
Odin, 10, 11, 19, 81
offerings, 70
Othel rune, 93
ox bones, 39

p

Pa Kua, 40, 41, 49
　Early Heaven Arrangement, 40, 42
　Later Heaven Arrangement, 40
Pages, 14, 15
　of Cups, 29, 35
　of Pentacles, 27
　of Swords, 23
　of Wands, 25
Pentacles (in Minor Arcana), 14, 15, 26-7
Peorth rune, 75, 88
Pi (in I Ching), 51, 52, 55
pip cards, 14
Pisces, 21
planets, 14
plant divas, 75
Pluto, 21
Po (in I Ching), 55
Prince (in Tarot), 14
Princess (in Tarot), 14
prophecy, 7
psychological insight, 7

q

Queen, 14, 15
　of Cups, 29
　of Pentacles, 27
　of Swords, 23
　of Wands, 25

r

Rad rune, 73, 73, 84
ribbon offering, 70
ritual, and consulting the I Ching, 10, 44
Romany spread, 36-7
rowan, and rune-making, 70
runecutters, 81
runemasters, 11, 71, 81
runes, 8, 67
　advanced divination, 76
　bindrunes, 79
　care of, 71
　Celtic Cross spread, 76
　cleansing, 71
　consulting the
　　drawing the runes, 69, 72, 72, 73
　　how divination works, 69
　　interpreting the runes, 69
　empowering, 71
　the four-element spread, 74, 78
　and healing, 11, 67, 77, 78
　history of, 68
　interpreting
　　interpretation of reversed runes, 72
　　meditating on a rune, 72
　　training the intuition with meditation, 72
　intuition and, 11, 71, 72, 79
　and learning, 67, 68
　making, 11, 67, 70
　and meditation, 10, 11, 72, 77, 77
　origin, 10
　personal rune, 11, 68
　reversed, 72
　rune magic, 77
　runes and their meanings, 81-93
　runic wishing ceremony, 79
　the single rune, 72, 72, 73
　storage, 71
　Thor's Hammer spread, 76
　the three-rune spread, 73
　tools and talismans, 79
　use by the shamans, 11
　using runes as an oracle, 75
　using runes to help others, giving a reading for someone else, 78
　vibrations, 11
　wearing, 77
　the world tree spread, 75
runic alphabets, 11, 71, 81

s

Sage (in I Ching), 44, 45, 50, 53-6, 58, 61
Sagittarius, 19
salt, 70, 71, 74
Saturn, 21
Scorpio, 19
seasons, 9-10
self-development, 42
Seven, 33
　of Cups, 29
　of Pentacles, 27
　of Swords, 23
　of Wands, 25
shamans, 7, 10, 11, 39, 75, 83
Shêng (in I Ching), 61
Shih (in I Ching), 51
Shih Ho (in I Ching), 55
Sigel rune, 89
singing, 78

Six, 33
　of Cups, 28, 35
　of Pentacles, 26
　of Swords, 22
　of Wands, 24
souls, 75
Spades, 14, 22
spirits, 70, 75
spring water, 71
staffs, 83
Star (in Major Arcana), 20, 33
stones, and rune-making, 70
Strength (in Major Arcana), 15, 19, 33
subconscious, 42, 68
Sui (in I Ching), 54
Sun
　(in I Ching), 43, 46, 47, 60, 64
　and the Major Arcana, 14, 21, 33
Sung (in I Ching), 51
supernatural entities, 75
Swords (in Minor Arcana), 14, 15, 22-3
synchronicity, 42

t

Ta Ch'u (in I Ching), 56
Ta Chuang (in I Ching), 58
Ta Kuo (in I Ching), 56
Ta Yu (in I Ching), 53
Tai (in I Ching), 52
Tai Chi, 40, 41
talismans, 79, 83
Tarot
　and intuition, 9, 13
　Major Arcana see Major Arcana
　Minor Arcana see Minor Arcana
　origin, 8
　reading the cards, 14, 31-7
　　the Celtic Cross spread, 34-5
　　how to read the tarot, 32
　　quick guides, 33
　　the Romany spread, 36-7
　"upright"/"reversed" meanings, 9, 14
Taurus, 17
Temperance (in Major Arcana), 19, 33
Ten, 33
　of Cups, 29
　of Pentacles, 27
　of Swords, 23
　of Wands, 25
Thor, 81
Thor's Hammer spread (runes), 76

Thorn rune, 83
Three, 33
　of Cups, 28
　of Pentacles, 26
　of Swords, 22
　of Wands, 24
three-rune spread, 73
Ting (in I Ching), 62
tobacco offering, 70
tortoise, 39, 42, 42
Tower (in Major Arcana), 20, 33
tree of knowledge, 10
　see also World Tree
trees, and runes, 11, 68, 70, 77
trigrams (in I Ching), 40, 41
　development, 42
　lower, 47, 49
　table of, 47
　upper, 47, 49
　Chen, 43, 47
　Chi'en, 43, 47
　K'an, 43, 47
　Ken, 43, 47

K'un, 43, 47
Li, 43, 47
Sun, 43, 47
Tui, 43, 47
Ts'ui (in I Ching), 61
Tui (in I Ching), 43, 46, 47, 64
Tun (in I Ching), 58
T'ung Jên (in I Ching), 53
Two, 33
　of Cups, 28
　of Pentacles, 26, 35
　of Swords, 22
　of Wands, 24
Tyr, 81, 90
Tyr rune, 73, 73, 75, 90

u

underworld, 75
upper world, 75

Ur rune, 82
Uranus, 16

v

Venus, 17
vibrations, 11, 68, 77, 78, 86
Vikings, 68
Virgo, 18

w

wands, 83
Wands (Minor Arcana), 14, 15, 24-5
Water element, 14, 15, 70, 74, 74, 92
Wei Chi (in I Ching), 65
Wen, Emperor, 40, 42
Wheel of Fortune (in Major Arcana), 18, 21, 33
Wilhelm, Richard, 42
willow, and rune-making, 70
wisdom
　ancient, 7
　of Odin, 10, 19
　and the world tree, 75
wishing, runic, 79
World (in Major Arcana), 21, 33
World Tree, 19, 70, 75, 81
　see also tree of knowledge
world tree spread (runes), 75
Wu Chi, 40
Wu Wang (in I Ching), 56
Wynn rune, 85

y

yang
　changing lines, 45
　and constructing a hexagram, 45
　gradations of, 41
　as a male quality, 10, 40
　old, 45
　and the seasons, 9
　single unbroken line, 40, 41
　the unifying principle, 40
　young, 45
yang-yang, 41
yang-yin, 41
yew, 70, 88
Yggdrasil, 10, 75, 81
yin
　changing lines, 45
　and constructing a hexagram, 45
　as a female quality, 10, 40
　gradations of, 41
　old, 45

　and the seasons, 9-10
　single broken line, 40, 41
　the unifying principle, 40
yin-yang, 41
yin-yin, 41
Yu (in I Ching), 53

z

zodiac signs, 14

Picture Acknowledgments:
The publishers would like to thank the following libraries for their permission to reproduce the pictures listed below:

BBC Natural History Unit: 40BL; 40L; 43TR.

Garden & Wildlife Matters Photo Library: 40B; 82TM; 84B; 86B; 87TM; 87BM; 88T; 88TM; 88B; 89BM; 89B; 90BM. 91TM; 91BM; 92BM; 93T; 93TM; 93B. Images Colour Library: 40TR; 40R; 40C; 76MR. Julie Meach: 43BMR. Natural Image: 43BL. Papilio Photographic: 89T; 93BM. Superstock: 90T. Tony Stone Images: 39MBL & 43MBL; 40BR; 43TL; 43MTL; 43MTR; 43BR; 82T; 82BM; 84; 86T. Werner Forman Archive: 75T. York Archaeological Trust: 88BM. AGM AGMüller for illustrations reproduced from IJJ Swiss Tarot Cards. © 1972 AGM AGMüller, CH-8212 Neuhausen, Switzerland.

Illustrations from Gendron, Pierpont Morgan Visconti-Sforza tarot decks, reproduced by permission of US Games System, Inc., Stamford CT. Images from Tarot of Marseille/I Tarocchi Marsigliesi reproduced by permission of Lo Scarabeo S.r.l. © Copyright 1996 Lo Scarabeo S.r.l., Corso Svizzera 31, 10143 Torino, Italy, all rights reserved, further reproduction prohibited. Illustrations from the ijj Swiss Tarot Cards, Tarot of the Old Path reproduced by permission of AGM AGMüller, CH-8212 Neuhausen, Switzerland © 1972 by AGM AGMüller, Switzerland.